PRAISE FOR *THE BUSH STILL BURNS*

"Don't miss this riveting account of Pastor Terry Mo(
tual journey. Starting as a mostly white Lutheran ch
they went beyond the standard church structure, be
community services, to the foreign realm of commu
those in the halls of power. They confronted city co
lords, and redlining banks and along the way created a unique
structure that everyone who wants to make a difference in the world should pay
attention to."

—**Jeff Merkley**, US senator for Oregon and former
member of Pastor Moe's congregation

"Terry Moe's vision, creativity, courage, authenticity, and collaborative spirit shim-
mer through the pages of this book—a primer in how to grow into formidable
spiritual leadership with our struggling neighboring communities and challenged
mainline congregations. Blending the wisdom of cutting-edge community organizing, ancient spiritual practices, and intentional congregational life, Pastor Moe's
work is and always has been well ahead of its time. As his bishop, I have seen
him become a beacon for many, many of our finest spiritual leaders in the Pacific
Northwest, a pillar of cloud by day and a pillar of fire by night, inviting us into the
hard transformational work of the gospel. How do we find Christ's resurrective
power in our lives, our spiritual communities, and our world? Read this! You will
discover a wise companion and mentor for your own journey."

—**Laurie Larson Caesar**, bishop of the Oregon Synod of
the Evangelical Lutheran Church in America (ELCA)

"This is a compelling story about what is possible when leaders are broken open
from the inside out to discover the mystery of God's transforming power in the
world through relationships with others. Over four decades of pastoral ministry, Terry Moe has been integrating spirituality and the practices of community
organizing to engage congregation and community with a view to discerning the
creative and redeeming activity of the Spirit. There is a good deal of practical wisdom here for how to do transformational ministry in this time between what the
church and world have been and the new reality that is trying to emerge."

—**Ray Pickett**, rector, Pacific Lutheran Theological Seminary

"An insightful, self-revelatory chronicle of Pastor Terry Moe's thirty-year odyssey
with his congregation in which both he and his faith community were transformed through contemplative organizing. A valuable resource for clergy and lay
leaders who are committed to courageous renewal for their congregations even if
the path requires the risk of entering into death and resurrection."

—**Dennis Jacobsen**, pastor, former director of the Gamaliel National Clergy
Caucus, and author of *A Spirituality for Doing Justice* (Fortress Press, 2021)

"Not every person sees fire along their path. Not every congregation organizes for
mission. Our gifts are unique. Our communities complex. *The Bush Still Burns* is
filled with the miracles of Christian mission. It is about the tenacious vision of one

pastor and the faithful journey of a single congregation. You will find your passions reflected here and your imagination pried open. Thank you, Terry Moe, for accompanying us through the wilderness."

—**Dave Brauer-Rieke**, former bishop of the Oregon Synod, ELCA, and project coordinator for the ELCA Region 1 Disaster Preparedness Project

"In a world threatened by kleptocracy and environmental plunder, Terry Moe harks back to the early rabbinic sentiment that God created and dismantled many worlds before arriving at this one. Courageously, his three decades' experience of taking apart and remaking his own parish links discerning political organizing with the discovery of Spirit outside the walls of church and synagogue. Like a bush on fire, he suggests, there are human stories waiting to be told, if we pay attention. We can go on worshiping tepidly, but his own humble narrative points us toward what's more incandescent: our wish to make the world more just and kind."

—**Joey Wolf**, rabbi emeritus at Havurah Shalom in Portland, Oregon

"Pastor Terry Moe weaves the stories of his life with the stories of his parishioners, colleagues, and friends into a narrative of his personal and professional journey and the gradual transformation and ultimate death and rebirth of the church he pastored for thirty-two years. With candor he describes his own and the congregation's successes and failures as they use tools of community organizing and practice of spirituality to engage in local community issues, like drug houses in the neighborhood or the financial burden city sewer development placed on homeowners, and confront the internal struggles of a dwindling blue-collar Lutheran congregation. Anyone concerned with the engagement of the church in the world or the need to transform church structures in our changing society should read this compelling memoir."

—**Monsignor Charles Lienert**, longtime pastor involved in community organizing and former vicar for clergy and pastoral planning in the Archdiocese of Portland in Oregon

"A must-read for local leaders of spirit communities and community organizers: how story-based relational organizing transformed a 1950s working-class Lutheran congregation and its pastor; how Terry Moe, with his people, engaged Scripture, ancient and modern spirituality, and public life; how, as a result, Redeemer faced its own death—and transformed into new life."

—**Dick Harmon**, former director for Industrial Areas Foundation Northwest

"Part memoir, part organizing primer, part spiritual wisdom, Terry Moe's beautiful storytelling invites us into what it means to act in the world as it is on behalf of the world as it should be. The depth of honesty in these pages shows us the best of courageous leadership, reminds us again that transformation is possible, and offers inspiration for all of us trying to lead the church in these complicated times."

—**Jessica Tate**, director, NEXT Church

THE
BUSH STILL
BURNS

THE
BUSH STILL
BURNS

HOW SPIRITUALITY
AND ORGANIZING
TRANSFORMED
A PASTOR AND
CONGREGATION

TERRY ALLEN MOE

FOREWORD BY SUSAN L. ENGH

FORTRESS PRESS
MINNEAPOLIS

To my wife,
Michelle Greenfield,
and family and in loving memory of my parents,
Arne and Sylvia Moe

And to all the leaders, members, friends
of Redeemer Lutheran, 1981–2013

CONTENTS

PART 4: Making a Way through the Wilderness

FOREWORD

In the fall of 2007, very early in my tenure as director for congregation-based organizing for the Evangelical Lutheran Church in America (ELCA), Rev. Terry Moe was the first leader to reach out and invite me to visit his congregation, Redeemer Lutheran in Portland, Oregon. At the time, I only knew *of* Terry; he had been a charter member of my predecessor's advisory team. In good leadership development form, Terry had already replaced himself on that team, in preparation for my tenure, with Wendy Hall, who was soon to become Redeemer/Enterbeing's first on-staff community organizer. But Terry was wise in asking me, our denomination's new organizing director, to come from Chicago to meet him and to learn what he and the church's leaders were up to, thus continuing to build strategic relationships with influencers in the ELCA.

When I got to Portland for that first visit, Terry had already filled my itinerary with close to a dozen one-to-ones with congregational and community leaders who all had some kind of stake in the ministry of Redeemer/Enterbeing. And he and those leaders were well prepared to give me an experiential taste of their ministry, exposing me to many of their typical meetings, activities, and actions. It was, as the saying goes, the beginning of a beautiful relationship, both with Pastor Moe and with the Redeemer / Leaven / Salt and Light community. I left Portland with a clearer vision of what this work I was now leading on a national scale could actually achieve on the ground, in people's lives and faith, and in the communities where they do ministry.

Terry had already been at this whole community-organizing business way longer than I had. It first "knocked on his door," as he tells it, in 1984. I discovered organizing in 1997 and through a different national network: he through Industrial Areas Foundation (IAF), I through Gamaliel. So when I first met Terry, though *he* was wisely cultivating a relationship with a brand-new denominational official, *I* was gaining a long-term mentor and coconspirator. Terry and I worked together often during the later years he describes in this book, as theological and ideological partners, as cotrainers, as program developers, and as builders of leadership and capacity.

For over thirty-five years, Rev. Moe has immersed himself in the methods and practices of faith- and broad-based organizing, enhancing and adapting them through his insatiable curiosity and in faithfulness to his pastoral call. While Terry's book invites us into some of the most intimate struggles of his personal and professional life, we get to see how those dynamics intertwine with the basic and more complex aspects of spirituality and organizing. Woven into this memoir of a pastor and faith community on a deep spiritual quest are the details of how he and his collaborators reconstructed a vital ministry on the foundations of community organizing.

In these pages, we discover how the "spiritual practice" of one-to-one relational meetings is the bread and butter of good organizing and congregational life. We witness the power of mentoring and being mentored, agitating and being agitated. We come to appreciate the wisdom of "when in doubt, form a team." We grasp the truth that "action is the oxygen of organizing." We learn how regular public evaluations can transform organizational culture for the better, developing strong leaders in the process. We recognize the beauty of getting to know and deeply care for not just one's own church members but also the neighbors, even the physical spaces, of one's ministry context. And in, with, and under it all, we can't help but come to the conclusion, as Terry and his partners did time and time again, that "we are the ones we've been waiting for."

How better than through stories from everyday lives and communities to grasp and grapple with what it takes—and how long it can take—to realize a vision that God has for the people of faith in a particular time and place? The journey is all the more compelling because of Terry's raw honesty and deep humility. Even as we travel with Terry on his spiritual quest and organizing journey, we find him coming to terms with his white male privilege. He continually challenges those dynamics by forging deep relationships with, and taking direction from, people of color. He intentionally mentors and collaborates with women, supervising several female pastoral interns, sharing power with female leaders, and co-orchestrating his own succession plan with a brilliant and powerful female pastor-organizer, Rev. Melissa Reed.

Besides our pastoral calls, theological curiosity, and affinity for organizing, another realm Terry and I each discovered at similar points along our timelines was adaptive leadership. We both realized, upon reading books by Sharon Daloz Parks and Ron Heifitz and by attending related courses and seminars, that adaptive-change principles dovetail beautifully with organizing practices. Partway into their journey, Terry and others around him began to grasp that, in order for congregational leaders and institutional partners to persist in applying the tools of organizing, they also needed to understand and make use of the dynamics of change theory.

Organizing can be transformational, but transformation can be difficult, even painful. And it can only happen over time, often long periods of it. Terry became so convinced that these two disciplines of organizing and adaptive leadership could be harnessed together for the greater good that he developed a curriculum blending the two. Then he leveraged relationships he had built over many years, with both faith and labor leaders, to bring together trainers and learners in order to strengthen our leadership in our respective realms. As the discipline prescribes, such endeavors are among the many experiments that adaptive leaders must dare to launch when "the old tried and true" just doesn't cut it for the challenges of the current era. This was and is Terry's self-assigned project upon "retiring" from pastoral ministry. Indeed, the bush still burns!

This book is at once a compelling account of a congregation's and its pastor's immersion in the Spirit of the Divine and the very human struggles and joys of cocreating a beloved community. I am a better pastor, organizer, and person for having known and worked with Rev. Terry Moe these many years, and his readers will be wiser, better equipped, and amply inspired by reading this book about his and Redeemer / Leaven / Salt and Light's thirty-five years and counting holy adventure.

Rev. Susan L. Engh
Retired ELCA director for faith-based community organizing
and author of *Women's Work: The Transformational
Power of Faith-Based Community Organizing*

PREFACE

The name *Moses* means "drawn from the water" in Hebrew, as many have noted. Fewer have noted that Moses is also an Egyptian name that means "born of —," with no antecedent. Ramses, for example (one can see the root of *Moses* in his name, *mses*) was born of the Egyptian god Ra. But who was Moses born of? Born of Jochebed, his biological mother? Born of his adoptive mother, the Egyptian princess Thermuthis? Born of Hebrew misery in slavery? Born of Egyptian grandeur and privilege? He was born a Hebrew slave. He was raised in Pharaoh's court. Moses was both Egyptian and Hebrew. He was a *both/and*. He discovered and acted upon his lineage and his calling, using both sides of his identity. He confirmed his Hebrew roots by killing an Egyptian overseer and burying him in the sand. When he was discovered, he became a refugee by fleeing to Moab. He was shepherding sheep in a foreign land when God mysteriously confronted him through a bush all aflame. Moses turned aside to pay attention. Why did this bush burn and yet was not consumed? From the heart of the fire, the voice of the Great I Am called him to liberate those in bondage in Egypt. In Egypt, Moses used his insider knowledge to outwit Pharaoh and win the freedom of his kin.

Redeemer Lutheran was also drawn from the waters of baptism in 1920 in Northeast Portland, Oregon. In many ways, it was a traditional mainline congregation, mostly white, mostly working class, mostly living in the "Egypt" of growing prosperity and comfort. The members of the congregation were second-generation immigrants. Many were transplants from the Midwest, many of whom came from Scandinavia and Germany.

Redeemer also had Hebrew roots in the story of Moses and the Exodus, though this was likely less clear to the people of the congregation. No one committed murder and fled. Instead, most just fell asleep as the world changed around them, becoming more and more oppressive and less and less like the world they wanted. In the 1980s and beyond, through a gradual process of spirituality and organizing, Redeemer turned aside to its own burning bush. It paid attention. It learned new practices. It deepened its life in the Spirit. It acted with others for a more just, equitable, and sustainable society through community organizing.

The story pales in comparison to the Exodus saga, but its inspiration is in the same root experience of discovering a bush all aflame that is not consumed. In its own small way, Redeemer was invited by a voice from a holy fire to lean into its own transformation. This is that story.

Part 1

MEETING THE BURNING BUSH

1981–1990

1 THE TRANSFORMATION BEGINS

Now Moses, tending the flock of his father-in-law Jethro, the priest of Midian, drove the flock into the wilderness, and came to Horeb, the mountain of God.[1]

—Exodus 3:1

Above all, trust the slow work of God. We are quite naturally impatient to reach the end without delay. We should like to skip the intermediate stages. We are impatient of being on the way to something unknown, something new. And yet it is the law of progress that it is made by passing through some stage of instability—and that it might take a very long time.[2]

—Pierre Teilhard de Chardin

IN JUNE 2013, REDEEMER LUTHERAN CHURCH, ESTABLISHED IN MAY 1920, ended its life. At the same time, a new organization named Leaven, a spiritually based, community-oriented membership nonprofit—and within it, a new ELCA[3] congregation, Salt and Light Lutheran Church—was born. It was necessary for Redeemer to break open for Leaven to be born. In a daring three-year campaign, which raised a million dollars to call a mission-developer pastor and a mission-developer organizer to work together, Redeemer wrestled with the angel of transformation, not knowing what was to come but realizing that continuing in the old way meant a slow and certain death.

[1] Exodus 3:1, *Hebrew-English Tanakh*, Jewish Publication Society, 1999 (hereafter JPS H-ET).
[2] Pierre Teilhard de Chardin, "Patient Trust," in *Hearts on Fire: Praying with Jesuits*, ed. Michael Harter, SJ (1993; repr., Chicago: Loyola, 2004), 102.
[3] Evangelical Lutheran Church in America.

This book is the story of how a pastor and congregation embraced a deep spirituality conjoined with community organizing in the IAF[4] tradition to shift, change, let go, and ultimately be transformed. It's the story of a traditional working-class congregation in a changed and changing neighborhood negotiating a narrow path of recovery. It's the story of a young second-call pastor falling simultaneously into a well of Spirit and a river of organizing going back to Moses. For over thirty years, the pastor and congregation together turned to face the burning bush and yet tried to not be consumed by it. Together they confronted the postmodern Egypt of the world and embraced a spirituality to strengthen, guide, and transform them.

Furthermore, this is a much larger story. It is the story of many congregations seeking to be relevant and vital in a rapidly changing world. The world has shifted out from under our churches, and most of us have been asleep. The world is less equitable. The world teeters on the brink of its own destruction through human-caused climate disruption. The rich are getting richer, and the poor are getting poorer. Could the church be awakened by embracing a deeper well of spirituality linked vitally to action through community organizing? Could the tandem of prayer and organizing be appealing to those who have given up on the church, who consider it judgmental and hypocritical, all talk and no action? Could a church connecting people's earthly values authentically in prayer and action be appealing to generations who have given up on religion?

Dietrich Bonhoeffer was the voice of an alternative church in the midst of a nazified church. He framed faithfulness as a way to love God and the world at the same time, to live fully in the world as it is, even as we work at making it as it could be in the vision of God. We do not live in Nazi Germany of the 1930s and 1940s. We do, however, live in a time of massive social and economic injustice, ecological devastation, and political uncertainty. How might the story

---

[4] IAF, formerly Industrial Areas Foundation, is one of several community-based organizing networks rooted in Saul Alinsky's Back of the Yards Neighborhood Council in Chicago in the 1940s.

of Moses's transformation from pastor to liberator beckon the church out of its drowsiness? In a way, the transformation of Redeemer is a minor story. I pray that it might ignite a larger fire in the hearts of the faithful to live with lives all aflame.

In June 2013, Redeemer died after ninety-three years. Today, Leaven Community / Salt and Light Lutheran Church lives. The transformation continues.

JANUARY 13, 1981: PASTOR YOUNG WHIPPERSNAPPER

The evening of my installation as pastor of Redeemer Lutheran in Portland, Oregon, I was getting on my robes to go into the sanctuary for the service when I heard a voice from down the hall: "Who's that young whippersnapper in the pastor's office?"

It was January 13, 1981. I was thirty years old. The voice, I would later learn, belonged to Vivian Richardson, a.k.a. Mrs. Richardson, a.k.a. Ms. Vivian, a.k.a. Queen Mother. Black, angry, articulate, and stubborn, she carried her thin, angular frame on the strength of defiance, garlic, and home remedies. I didn't know it then, but I would come to understand that she was deserving of the title "African queen" as well. I would come to love her, but only after struggling to get past the prickliness and well-worn armor that had served her well through Jim Crow and into this decade. As my persona was emerging from the fjords and lefse of my Nordic culture into a broader, more complex world, I came to see and love her as she was, despite—and maybe because of—the way she pointed her bony finger in an accusatory manner at me and other whites when she talked. I came to discover, know, and accept a deeper part of myself, ugly in many ways and hidden, but not from

> In June 2013, Redeemer died after ninety-three years. Today, Leaven Community / Salt and Light Lutheran Church lives. The transformation continues.

her. It was like she held a black light up to my body, revealing the wrinkles of my whiteness and highlighting the distance between our lives while at the same time resolutely knowing and loving me in return. It was she who schooled us in Afro Sheen for our adopted son's hair.

She was but one of many people I came to know and love from Redeemer and the community in which we lived. Together we turned to a burning bush and pondered, *What can this be?* Together, but not without struggle, we realized that we were falling into God and the world at the same time.

JUNE 30, 2013: "THANK YOU, LORD"

My last Sunday at Redeemer—thirty-two years, five months, and seventeen days after my installation—Vivian was already sleeping with the ancestors. I imagined her pointing her bony finger at the rainbow faces in white robes singing to the Lamb who makes all things new. As I looked out at the congregation for the last time, I slipped myself into the back row of the choir with a microphone in my hand for the offering song. I'm not a singer by any standard, but I chose to brave a solo that day. I sang a spiritual often sung in Black churches, "Thank You, Lord":

> Thank you, Lord. Thank you, Lord. Thank you, Lord.
>   I just want to thank you, Lord.
> Been so good. Been so good. Been so good.
>   I just want to thank you, Lord.

I felt like I was joining the angels around the Lamb, singing to those present and those in the beyond who had walked with me across deserts and dangerous valleys, who had come to know and love me with bonds of mutual affection, a beloved community. I was singing to Vivian. I was singing to the nearly two hundred elders I buried as their pastor. These people who once were like cardboard cutouts in the pews became full of texture and depth, breath, and blood—some more than others, some just as a glimpse in my experience, but all a great cloud of witnesses, my own parents among them, as well as our first granddaughter, Angelique, stillborn in 1994. I was singing to the dancing bones of Ezekiel's prophecy, a community rising in hope.

Most especially, I was singing "Thank You, Lord" to the source of the awakening in my own soul, for the Spirit and community's transformative work in my being. Not completely, not perfectly, but visibly, as if through a dim glass, I was seeing myself anew, and the congregation, once made of old wineskins, was now ready for new wine. The stories of my own transformation, the transformation of the congregation, and the ongoing transformation of the Spirit here and everywhere came together as I took my leave of Redeemer in three words: "Thank You, Lord." I had drunk deeply of the cup of transformation at the heart of creation, at the center of love and justice, and was filled with faith, hope, and love even as I shed tears of sorrow at leaving.

THE BUSH BURNS IN SPIRITUALITY AND ORGANIZING

Between Vivian's voice in the hallway in 1981 and my version of "Thank You, Lord" in 2013, Redeemer Lutheran turned to a burning bush that called us to a deepening, engaged spirituality and community organizing in the tradition of the IAF. Just as Moses turned aside, listened, and was called to confront the power of Egypt, Redeemer was called to confront our contemporary Egypt. We came to feel the heat. We pondered the tentacles of flame in our hearts and in our community. We wondered, *Why doesn't the bush burn up?* We prayed. We organized. We faced the pharaohs of our times. We confronted the Egypt we carried in our own national and church culture.

The spirituality we embraced was in many ways very traditional. We learned from Christian mystics, ancient and modern. We prayed in Sunday liturgy and learned to pray in silence, in meditation, and in contemplation. We learned to pray with and for one another. In tandem with organizing, we fell into God and the world at the same time. Individual meetings, also called one-to-ones or relational meetings, became a spiritual practice alongside and eventually within the liturgy. Listening deeply not only to members but to our neighbors and the broader community brought new prayers. Reflection, evaluation, strategic planning, actions at city hall, and negotiations with corporate leaders led Redeemer out of itself and into the whole world God so loves.

Being a church got complicated. And it got interesting. The transformation didn't happen overnight. Nobody saw Leaven as it came to be when Redeemer gave itself over to a new mission to build a larger and more powerful spiritual community with and alongside Redeemer. Nobody foresaw that the beginning of this new mission would be the end of Redeemer. That part came gradually. It didn't happen in a flash of light, though the burning bush became ever clearer, having been there all along. The real miracle is not the outcome of an innovative new community with a Lutheran congregation as an integral part. The real miracle is that Redeemer turned to face the burning bush and ventured forth not knowing the future.

> The real miracle is that Redeemer turned to face the burning bush and ventured forth not knowing the future.

In a well-funded, three-and-a-half-year campaign from February 2010 until June 30, 2013, Redeemer turned itself over to a whole new entity, Leaven Community, a larger, spiritual, member-based nonprofit overarching and including a new congregation of the Evangelical Lutheran Church in America (ELCA), Salt and Light Lutheran Church.

In June 2013, Redeemer died. Today, Leaven / Salt and Light lives. The bush still burns.

FOR REFLECTION

Chapter 1 reflects on the beginning and the end of a ministry. The rest of the story is told in the following chapters.

- Where are you and where is your faith community in terms of a beginning, a middle, and an end? What makes you say this?
- How are you currently thinking about this stage or all these stages?

2 BURNING BUSH: THE FIRE OF SPIRITUALITY AND ORGANIZING

An angel of the Lord appeared to him in a blazing fire out of a bush. He gazed, and there was a bush all aflame, yet the bush was not consumed.[1]

—Exodus 3:2

To awaken spiritually means that we develop a new awareness of God's energy in the world in order to discern what is needed to open the possibilities for human flourishing.[2]

—Diana Butler Bass

Real-world organizations not only have members, leaders, and staff; they also have organizers (acknowledged or not) whose function is to increase the active participation of members and to create the conditions in which strong new leaders emerge.[3]

—Richard Rothstein

PASTOR YOUNG WHIPPERSNAPPER, INDEED!

AS AN EAGER YOUNG PASTOR, I FELT IMMEDIATELY CALLED TO CHANGE THE congregation. I had my master of divinity degree and five years of parish experience. The congregation had seen a rapid decline and

---

[1] Exodus 3:2, JPS H-ET.
[2] Diana Butler Bass, *Christianity after Religion: The End of Church and the Beginning of a New Spiritual Awakening* (New York: HarperCollins, 2012), 37.
[3] Richard Rothstein, "What Is an Organizer (1973)," in *People Power: The Community Organizing Tradition of Saul Alinsky*, ed. Aaron Schutz and Mike Miller (Nashville, TN: Vanderbilt University Press, 2015), 46.

clearly seemed to pin their hopes for the future on me as a young upstart pastor. It was a thin gruel for transformation. If the impulse to change was correct, my capacity to lead was totally lacking. I forged ahead. First, I sent out funeral preference forms in the newsletter to every family. I saw so much gray in the congregation, I figured they needed to prepare their funerals right away, not realizing that many were in their early sixties. I got two back, one from the chaplain at Emanuel Hospital, a dear saint and one of the first women ordained in the Lutheran Church, and one from a sweet couple who would have walked on fire for the pastor of their church. After a few years, I proposed a sanctuary redesign, shifting pews to face the east windows in a semicircle and putting an altar in the middle. In my view, this would provide for a closer community. Though the council approved the plan, members at the annual meeting resoundingly defeated the proposal; I think it was one in favor (me!) and a hundred against. Even the council members who had approved it spoke against it publicly. It was as close to a tar-and-feathering experience as I ever wanted to come. I was humiliated. I had little understanding of what had just happened.

It's been said that the congregation is one of the most complex social and organizational systems, and I fell headlong into the pit of that reality. Clearly, I had much to learn. I certainly could have benefited from the wisdom of Reinhold Niebuhr, who in his first parish in 1915 wrote, "There is something ludicrous about a callow young fool like myself standing up to preach a sermon to these good folks. I talk wisely about life and know little about life's problems. I tell them of the need for sacrifice, although most of them could tell me something about what that really means."[4]

I could easily have resigned from Redeemer following this catastrophic annual meeting in January 1984. But for reasons I don't fully understand, I stayed. Laid low. I licked my wounds. Mysteriously—and at just the right time—I was opened to a significant new life in the

---

[4] Reinhold Niebuhr, *Leaves from the Notebook of a Tamed Cynic* (Louisville, KY: Westminster / John Knox, 1990), 9.

form of prayer and organizing. The bush was all aflame and not consumed.

It didn't happen overnight. It happened in fits and starts, in bursts of new energy and troubling obstacles. Together we learned to turn aside in prayer and organizing to engage, suffer, work, strategize, debrief, plan, listen, pray, and stay together.

FALLING INTO THE BLACK WORLD

The Albina Ministerial Alliance (AMA), the Black clergy association in Portland, was formed in 1972 out of racial tension in the 1960s and 1970s. There I met two Black pastors who invited me into the Black church world, a world I had only known from the outside. Simultaneously, Black members of the congregation like Vivian Richardson took me under their wings. While learning the complexities of the congregation in a changing neighborhood, I began to fall into the Black world, a world much more akin to the biblical Egypt of Moses's day in its richness and suffering.

Rev. John Jackson was the pastor of Mount Olivet Baptist, a historic Black congregation in Portland located near Veterans Memorial Coliseum, home of the Portland Trail Blazers, the building that displaced hundreds of Black families along with the adjacent development of Emanuel Hospital. Rev. Jackson raised a strong voice in his role as president of AMA in coalition with Ron Herndon, community activist and cochair with Rev. Jackson of the Black United Front. Rev. Jackson was the good cop, negotiating with school and city officials, while Ron danced on the tables of power. Together they created hope for a community dwarfed by whiteness in the whitest city in America. Beside Rev. Jackson was Rev. John Garlington of Maranatha Church, a strong, charismatic congregation located just a mile from Redeemer. The two Johns took me in. I became the secretary of AMA. I marched with them down Union Avenue, eventually renamed Martin Luther King Jr. Boulevard, in solidarity with those who lived in neglect and surrounded by blight in the backyards of

Portland. Redeemer, though mostly white, was also inside the invisible red lines determining neighborhood stability, though we escaped the added indignities of race—for the most part.

In 1985, Tony Stevenson, a Black off-duty security guard, was confronted by Portland police. A scuffle ensued as officers restrained Stevenson with a carotid artery hold, meant to subdue him. Instead, he suffocated and died. AMA organized a march to city hall. I joined them. Along the way, Rev. Jackson invited me to "say a few words" when we got to city hall. Following several headliner Black clergy, I found my way to the microphone and added words from Amos 5:15:

> Hate evil and love good,
>   and establish justice in *the gate*.

It was my first public preaching, a calling I was falling into and would find myself practicing more and more as I got engaged in the community. The march was one of many, I would learn. Later that same week, the TV news showed Portland police celebrating and passing out T-shirts in their locker room that said, "Smoke 'Em, Don't Choke 'Em." I couldn't believe the hurtful words that aligned me, a white pastor, with a legacy of violence in proximity to the slavery forced upon the Hebrew people by ancient Egypt's power structure, even as I stood shoulder to shoulder with the Black AMA clergy.

The AMA wasn't my only connection with the Black community, though it was pivotal. Closer to home, I got to know and love the Black families of Redeemer, people who had joined Redeemer long before I arrived.

BEN WEBB

I met Ben, a tall Black man, when I first came to Portland to interview for the vacancy at Redeemer. At the time, he was the community outreach coordinator for Concordia University and was asked by Redeemer leadership to show me around Portland while I was there.

I spent a lot of time with Ben, and as I learned his story in bits and pieces, I came to love him dearly. He was one of the most interesting people I ever met.

While serving in the Navy, he fell from a tower, crushing his jaw and breaking his leg. He talked and smiled a bit from the side of his mouth, just enough to notice. His limp and his slightly twisted face merely added to his charm and distinction. In the early 1950s, he sought to desegregate lunch counters and worship services in Portland through the St. Martin de Porres Society, a Black Catholic organization. The more I learned from Ben, the more I appreciated his gentle, kind spirit; his listening, probing demeanor at church meetings; and his wisdom forged in long suffering. Ben was a Renaissance man who loved Shakespeare and the classics, had a degree in economics from the University of Oregon, and loved civil war history. He served on the Emanuel Hospital and Oregon Health Sciences University Ethics Committees, reading and discussing complicated cases with physicians and other experts.

In the early 1960s, he began to reach again beyond his Southern Baptist upbringing by exploring the Unitarian congregation next to the large downtown Baptist congregation. It was here, in adjacent church parking lots, that he met Viola, a white and Finnish former Lutheran exploring the more expressive Baptist tradition. Because interracial marriage was illegal in Oregon and Washington—along with seventeen other, mostly southern states—Ben and Vi drove to Vancouver, British Columbia, in 1963 to be married. I realized later that they were married four years prior to the important film depicting an interracial marriage, *Guess Who's Coming to Dinner* (1967), featuring Sidney Poitier and Katharine Houghton as the interracial couple and Katharine Hepburn and Spencer Tracy as the white parents coming to grips with it.

Ben and Vi were courageous pioneers not only in their social and spiritual journeys but socially and politically as well. Vi told me she had *sisu*, a toughness of soul formed in Finnish people who survived the precarious border of Russia. Or as Wikipedia defines it, "A Finnish concept described as stoic determination, tenacity of purpose, grit, bravery, resilience, and hardiness."[5] Black determination and purposeful energy united with a *sisu* soul undaunted.

Soon after their marriage, they moved to Tanzania to serve in the United States Agency for International Development (USAID). It was in Tanzania that their daughter, Damaris, was born. She was tall and beautiful like her mother and father, and her unique mocha complexion was a rich mix of Finnish and Black lineages. I watched her graduate from Jefferson High School, a predominantly Black public school in Portland. Damaris took advantage of the dance and drama magnet at Jefferson to propel her to New York University, where she majored in drama, becoming an off-Broadway playwright and producer in New York, where she lived for the next twenty years before returning home to Portland as her parents aged. In Portland, she wrote, produced, and starred in a one-act play, *The Box Marked Black*, about her mixed-race heritage. She called herself "mulato" despite that term's speckled history. She claimed her mixed heritage and carried forward both the *sisu* of her Finnish mother and the steadfast determination of her Black father.

Visiting the home of Ben and Vi was like stepping into another world. An African drum served as a coffee table, and carved artifacts surrounded the living room, totems both listening to and participating in the many conversations the space invited. They had lived in Africa twice, first in Tanzania and later in Botswana. One year we held multiple sessions in their home, crowding seventeen people—Black, white, and mixed—into a tiny space to discuss Isabel Wilkerson's *The Warmth of Other Suns: The Epic Story of America's Great Migration*,[6] a beautiful and timely book covering the migrations of Black folk from the South to the North, Midwest, and West.

> Visiting the home of Ben and Vi was like stepping into another world.

---

[5] Wikipedia, s.v. "Sisu," last modified June 27, 2020, 14:52. http://en.wikipedia.org/wiki/Sisu.
[6] Isabel Wilkerson, *The Warmth of Other Suns: The Epic Story of America's Great Migration* (New York: Vintage, 2010).

In Ben and Vi's crowded living room, Black folks described their own journeys, inspired by the stories in the book, so parallel to their own. And white folks began to also share their migration stories from Germany, Finland, Russia, Scandinavia, and more to America, first to the East and Midwest and eventually to Portland. They were pushed by forces that also drove the migration of Black families between 1910 and 1970, but their experiences lacked the racist elements.

Ben spoke sparingly of his upbringing and early years, though during a series of conversations at Redeemer, he was paired with a white woman around his same age, also a longtime member, whose migration had taken her to Portland from a North Dakota farm after World War II. The assigned relational meeting question was "How, when, and why did you come to Portland?" Easy enough. Everybody has a story about that! Ben shared how his family packed a four-day supply of bologna sandwiches and slept in the car on the way from Chicago to Portland, where his dad, a Baptist missionary, was to establish a new church. On hearing his story, Alice remarked, "You must have been poor," to which Ben replied gently, "No, we were Black." Only then did he reveal the hidden truth of his story: no restaurant or motel along the way would accommodate his family. She was shocked. It was only one of many, many conversations over the years that began to knit our community together while simultaneously revealing the painful cracks and chasms self-evident to folks of color but seldom as evident to whites.

Ben loved to cook. When he wanted to talk, he would invite me over for waffles in their cozy kitchen nook, where among a scattering of *New York Times* papers and letters opened or not, he would serve coffee and steaming waffles with real maple syrup. Ben had nieces and nephews and their families in the area. He was the main chef for family dinners and often prepared food for Thanksgiving and Christmas gatherings. One Christmas morning, he was starting the turkey and preparing the fixings when he noticed it was getting late—even for Vi—to be still sleeping. When he went up to wake her, she lay quietly in the bed, having suffered a massive stroke. She died two days later on December 27, 2009.

Ben grieved hard as he suffered the loss of his most precious Vi. He often told me that he expected to die first, that he was ready. He had a history of congestive heart failure and was hospitalized several times before Vi died. Not too long after her death, however, he started to cook for others who were also grieving—one recently divorced, another who had experienced the loss of a job, another not finding peace with the addiction of her grandson, another reeling from the death of his spouse as well. Ben started cooking for two or three, and the groups grew to ten or twelve. He cooked monthly, and people sat around his big dining room table, like he had planned to do with Vi and family that Christmas Day. Afterward, in the cramped living room occupied by the African totems, and now also the spirits of the dead, they would talk—or not—about their losses. Ben's cooking and hospitality brought comfort and release to many, not least of all to himself. He called it the "Grief and Eat" group, another expression of this amazing, wonderful man, Ben Webb.

I came back for Ben's memorial in October 2014. Redeemer was now Salt and Light Lutheran, but when Pastor Reed invited me to copreside, I deferred, both to give her space and because I wanted my own space to grieve for Ben, away from my pastor role. I had loved Ben as his pastor, but I wanted to grieve my mentor and friend. He told me once, as the vision for Leaven / Salt and Light began to unfold and manifest its sparkling reality, "This is what I always wanted in a church." I'll never forget that. Like Simeon, he saw the fulfillment of a dream. Ben was one of the fortunate leaders who got to participate in its transformation even as he was being transformed.

THE FALL OF SPIRITUALITY AND THE SPRING OF ORGANIZING

As I was drawn into the Black community and the Redeemer world more deeply, my role as pastor and leader began to shift. I can describe it as a fall, because it was only partly volitional. Mostly it was by the grace of God and the skin of my knees.

The fall in Oregon is a beautiful, if mournful, time of year. The wind begins to blow more coldly as the days shorten, unnoticeably at first, like the first signs of aging, then more forcefully as the full wet and cold rains come. Trees that had, it seems, only moments earlier burst into leaf now begin to show their fiery dying orange and dull brown. The fall season had set in when I saw and responded to a flyer across my desk that read, "Introduction to Spiritual Living," offered by the Grotto, a sacred shrine and sanctuary run by a small Servite monastery. I was inspired to give it a try.

For twenty weeks, I was a first-grader again among mostly sisters, lay and religious, learning to pray. For twenty weeks from October 1983 until May 1984, every Tuesday afternoon from two until four, I learned prayer practices: journaling, meditation, spiritual reading (lectio), contemplation, centering prayer, silence, guided meditation, and spiritual direction—all bright new leaves on my growing prayer tree. It marked a new beginning. The fall of 1983 was a kind of spring for me. I fell heart-long into a well of spirituality.

The spring in Oregon feels much like the fall. The wind blows surprisingly cold, carrying sheets of rain from the ocean with amazing regularity and ease. It is hard to recognize the new signs of life among the drabness of gray showers. The drenched earth sputters, near drowning, and then with loud gasps, it seems in one day of creation to bring the color of daffodils and tulips to light, a miracle repeated over and over again and yet mesmerizing each time it occurs. In the spring of 1984, Kevin Jeans-Gail, called by the Catholic Campaign for Human Development to explore an interest in community organizing, sat in the big green chair near my desk and listened to my story. Was the world as I wanted it? Of course not. But my idealism left me frustrated because there was no bridge between my present turmoil and the vision that was beginning to flower within me. "You can't get from here to there by yourself," he said, "What's your first step?" So began on a cloudy spring day in Oregon my journey into community organizing.

In the fall of 1983 and the spring of 1984, within arm's reach of each other, I encountered a burning bush in the form of classical

> I encountered a burning bush in the form of classical Christian spirituality and IAF community organizing.

Christian spirituality and IAF community organizing. Over the years, spirituality and organizing became tongues of a common fire that raged relentlessly in me and in the congregation, searing away the old and bringing a transformation we never dreamed of. We turned aside to see this bush that blazed without burning out. In time the gentle waters of baptism, unfolding decently and in good Lutheran order, joined the boundless wells of mystics and the raging waters of justice.

INTRODUCTION TO SPIRITUAL LIVING

I hadn't realized how famished I had become until a flyer, "Introduction to Spiritual Living," blew across my desk. I realized it was something I had longed for since my childhood. After nearly ten years as an ordained Lutheran pastor and two decades after my own baptism, I fell into an ocean of spirituality and discovered the depth of the tradition I loved yet hadn't fully experienced.

A young Servite novice named Steve Coffey led the Introduction to Spiritual Living class. He and I were about the same age. We were the youngest in the class and the only men as well. I was introduced to many ways to pray, practiced them with the group, and experimented at home. I learned several prayer practices (see above). This class at the Grotto provided a great awakening of my spiritual self. I ate it up. As we read the mystics and prayed the variety of mystical experiences, my heart began to swell and open. How I longed for the living God! Scales fell from my eyes. My heart, like a spring, pulsed with new waters up through my neck to my head, fragile and tentative at first, then like a stream through my body and beyond. Like Moses, I turned aside to see the burning bush and wondered why it was not consumed. I was beginning what some have called the longest human journey—from my head to my heart.

SPIRITUAL DIRECTION

The very next fall, October 1984, I joined a two-year class in spiritual direction taught by the same Servite novice, who this time partnered with a nun, Sister Sylvia, to co-lead the group. I wasn't really interested in becoming a spiritual director; I didn't even know what a spiritual director was, but I was eager to go deeper in prayer and meditation. Whatever I got from the "Introduction to Spiritual Living," I wanted more. I ached, I pined, I longed, I thirsted—for what? Why was this happening to me now when I was thirty-four years old? What was this holy longing I was feeling and could not let rest?

During this second class, I met a serene and sturdy Benedictine nun, Sister Antoinette, who taught a section on Lectio Divina for the spiritual direction class. When it was time to get a spiritual director, I asked her, not knowing what a lifesaving and long-lasting relationship this would become. For the next thirty years, every four to six weeks, I drove an hour along the Willamette River to the Shalom Prayer Center on the grounds of the Queen of Angels Monastery, established in the late 1800s by stalwart sisters from Switzerland. Sister Antoinette had joined the community from her South Dakota home when she was nineteen. She developed the Benedictine Nursing Home, becoming the prioress for several terms, and only recently had opened the Shalom Prayer Center. During the years I met with her, she survived breast cancer, which included surgery, chemotherapy, and weekly radiation appointments. She told me it was her "year of cancer." When she was done, she was done.

She referred to such times as phases: "My novitiate phase, my phase of developing the nursing center, my two terms as prioress, my Notre Dame phase when I learned more about the spirituality I had been practicing for twenty-five years, my Shalom Prayer Center phase, my cancer stage, my wisdom phase."

Sister Antoinette helped me think about my own life and ministry in phases. What was I building? What phase was I in? What was done and what was just beginning? What was I ready to leave behind? What new thing was on the horizon?

Driving through the fields of the Willamette Valley to visit Sister Antoinette, I passed vineyards and fields of hops for the burgeoning wine and beer microenterprises. They replaced or stood alongside soy, wheat, and oats fields, with intermittent dairies dotting the landscape. As I drove through this fertile landscape, I entered more completely into the spiritual world. Each season reminded me of the rhythms of my own life and the rhythms of my deepening spiritual life. I contemplated how the gnarled old grape vines in winter in their seventieth year looked like crusty, lifeless castaways, and then by summer, they looked green and full of life. The powerful visual testimony of the fields and vineyards spoke to the latent potential of my winter moments, times when growth and new life seem so far away.

The Shalom Prayer Center was a place apart from the inner city where I lived and worked. I talked to Sister Antoinette about everything—my family, what was going on at Redeemer, organizing—and mostly she would simply listen. "How have you brought that to prayer?" she might ask. Or "What might God be inviting you to?" I can remember only one time she actually directed me, pointing a wizened finger at me and with authority pronouncing, "Don't do that." I don't even remember what it was about, but I listened. Mostly she accompanied me, and I grew to love her. When I planned my first sabbatical in 1990, I looked across the country for places to do a thirty-day directed retreat. I had set aside funds to go anywhere in the US but ended up doing the "Prayer of the Heart" retreat at Mount Angel with Sister Antoinette as my director.

AND THEN THERE WAS ORGANIZING

If this newly discovered ancient and time-tested spirituality was one pathway to opening a whole new world for me, another portal of renewal was community organizing. I fell into spirituality quite by chance in the fall of 1983, but my introduction to organizing literally knocked on my door in the person of Kevin Jeans-Gail, the young organizer hired by the Catholic Campaign for Human Development to explore interest in community organizing in Portland. In the spring of 1984, not six months after starting my first introductory course at the Grotto, I skidded cautiously into organizing. As in my encounter with spirituality, I was a newbie, a wannabe, a beginner. Like my plunge into spirituality, my encounter with organizing was steep and rapid, though the trajectory of learning and integrating took years, even decades. Spirituality and organizing overlapped for me at their beginnings; they would intertwine restlessly for the rest of my life. I was moving down a steep curve of discovery and transformation.

Kevin Jeans-Gail was a one-of-a-kind person. My wife quipped that he had hatched from an alien pod instead of being born. As I would later learn, organizers are rare and uniquely gifted for thinking and acting outside the box. They question. They agitate. They do not accept all the rules. In some ways, they literally live in another world, the world that ought to be. He was a mirror image of Sister Antoinette. Both were devout Catholics. One was older, feminine, rural, from a small town in the Midwest, cloistered, slow to judge, and reserved. The other was young, male, married, urban, from South

Philly, quick to jump, and outgoing. In many ways, they personi-
fied the divergent gifts of spirituality and organizing that I was now
engaging in.

I liked Kevin. His persistence and passion were attractive. He
didn't sell me but rather invited me. I was cautious. Already my plate
was full. I was participating in Ecumenical Ministries of Oregon, an
innovative cooperative of denominations doing all kinds of social
service and advocacy. I was deeply engaged in AMA, the local African
American clergy association as well. How could I possibly take on
something else? Over time, I would choose paths that would both
rip me away from valuable ministries and relationships and plant me
deeply in the soil of congregation-based organizing that demanded
increasing commitment.

Month after month, he sat in my office skillfully confronting
me with provocative questions: "So are you satisfied with the way
things are in your congregation and neighborhood?" "What are you
spending your time on and why?" "What other pastors and leaders
do you know and work with?" And eventually, "What would it be
like for you to meet other pastors who might be interested in going
upstream to address some of the root causes of what you and your
members are experiencing?"

I did meet interesting priests and lay leaders who took their faith
seriously, who listened to the cries of their community and acted. I
met Father Chuck Lienert at Immaculate Heart near Emanuel Hospital; Father Jack Mosbrucker at St. Charles, a mile east of Redeemer;
and Father Bob Krueger, who for many years served St. Andrew,
the dynamic and mixed-race parish nearest Redeemer. Pastor John
Rodgers, Vernon Presbyterian, became a key colleague as organizing
brought us together. Catholic women found ways to lead within their
system. Sister Phyllis, a Holy Names nun, and pastoral associates
Valerie Chapman and Chris Kresek joined Protestant lay leaders
like Nancy Phelps and others too numerous to name. Alongside the
organizing work, we formed a prayer circle to pray and reflect on our
experiences as called organizing leaders.

Could it be God calling us to see the burning bush in the cries of the people in our community? Might the Holy One who knows the sufferings of all be coming down to do something about it? What did the Almighty and All-Tender One see on the streets of the world? What decisions were being discussed in the Divine Council around its own table of power? Did the congregation named Redeemer have a clue? Were we, who had begun to feel the heat of the burning bush, being invited to listen to our own pain and the cries of others? Were we being called to do something about it?

> Could it be God calling us to see the burning bush in the cries of the people in our community?

Kevin provided for me the first glimmer of the power of the individual meeting, a face-to-face, provocative conversation that explores interests and agitates values dormant or hidden in unreflective busyness. At first, I was mostly on the receiving side. As I learned the arts and practices of organizing, these initial conversations and the training that followed began to generate significant relationships with other key leaders who would change my life forever. At the very same time that spirituality was unfolding for me, catching me up in a long-term spiral of development, I leaned more intentionally into community organizing. I attended weekend training sessions with other clergy and lay leaders taught by Mike Miller,[7] an experienced organizer from San Francisco. I met regularly with Kevin. Eventually my interest caught fire.

Turning aside as a pastor in the wilderness of Portland, I heard a voice straining to be heard through my white, working-class upbringing. In encountering Steve Coffey and Sister Antoinette, I found mentors in my spiritual quest. In Kevin and Mike Miller, I was found by mentors of a different sort, one Catholic and one Jewish, who worked with me to open me to a wider, more complex world. I didn't leap or

---

[7] See also Miller and Schutz, eds., *People Power.*

spring into organizing as much as I was lured, goaded, and enchanted until I couldn't turn back.

In time, the congregation I served would apply these lessons within our own congregation. A broad and deepening spirituality and a vigorous engagement in community organizing would transform us. At this point, you may well wonder, What happens to people who pray *and* organize? What impact can community organizing have on one's spiritual life? What does a spiritual life have to do with organizing? How are life and God and relationships changed by intentional engagement with prayer and organizing? How can a journey of prayer and organizing lead to important discoveries and discernment? How can visions and concrete practices drawn from the wells of prayer and organizing encourage, teach, and lead those who seek transformation and justice? These are questions that I and the Redeemer Church were going to face in our journey through the wilderness together.

FOR REFLECTION

Chapter 2 tells the initial story of how spirituality and organizing came together for the pastor and congregation.

- What is your story of prayer/spirituality? Where you are now?
- How has your story of spirituality/prayer moved or changed?
- What is your story of social engagement?
- How has your story of social engagement moved or changed?

3 TURNING ASIDE: THE BUSH ALL AFLAME

Moses said, "I must turn aside to look at this marvelous sight; why doesn't the bush burn up?"[1]

—Exodus 3:3

Spirituality is not to be learned in flight from the world, by fleeing from things to a place of solitude; rather we must learn to maintain an inner solitude regardless of where we are or who we are with. We must learn to penetrate things, and find God there.[2]

—Meister Eckhart

That is, today's complex conditions require acts of leadership that assist people in moving beyond the edge of familiar patterns into the unknown terrain of greater complexity, new learning, and new behaviors, usually requiring loss, grief, conflict, risk, stress, and creativity.[3]

—Sharon Daloz Parks

PORTLAND ORGANIZING PROJECT (POP), A CONGREGATION-BASED ORGANIZING ENTITY

KEVIN JEANS-GAIL HAD NOT ONLY BEEN KNOCKING ON MY DOOR BUT meeting regularly with interested clergy and lay leaders throughout

---

[1] Exodus 3:3, JPS H-ET.

[2] Meister Eckhart quoted in Kester Brewin, *Signs of Emergence: A Vision for Church That Is Organic/Networked/Decentralized/Bottom-Up/Communal/Flexible (Always Evolving)* (Grand Rapids, MI: Baker, 2007), 132.

[3] Sharon Daloz Parks, *Leadership Can Be Taught* (Boston: Harvard Business Press, 2005), 9.

working-class Portland. Now a team of faith leaders strategically invited congregations from the east side of Portland, where most of the poorer and working-class people lived, to discern if, how, and when a congregation-based organization would make sense. These congregations and neighborhoods did not show up on the maps of the powerful, nor were they represented at the tables of decision makers. It took time. After more than a year of conversations, trainings, leader sessions, and congregational and church council votes, eight congregations committed to forming the Portland Organizing Project (POP). Redeemer was number nine.

Further training instigated listening seasons inside congregations to identify issues and discover interested leaders. POP led campaigns to address issues upstream that were impacting people in our neighborhoods based on the stories heard in our congregations and neighborhoods. POP's purpose was not protest. It was not advocacy on behalf of others. POP existed to act directly on local decision makers to change things for the better.

The world continued to kick our community to the side of the road. The first issue POP took on was drug houses. At the time, hundreds of drug houses were blighting particular neighborhoods, many in the neighborhoods where our congregations gathered. Redeemer lay smack-dab in the middle of a dangerous neighborhood shared by St. Andrew and St. Charles on either side and Vernon Presbyterian up the street. Leaders made up of teams of pastors and lay leaders from POP congregations met with local police and learned the lessons of power: "Power concedes nothing without demand." "No permanent allies, no permanent enemies." "Power that is given can be taken back; power that is built lasts."

> We learned to start at the top of the ladder of power, to meet with the highest-ranking decision maker we could garner.

We learned to start at the top of the ladder of power, to meet with the highest-ranking decision maker we could garner, because meeting with lesser officials was often a frustrating runaround. Sometimes we had to work our way up.

One of our first meetings in the drug house campaign was with a police sergeant. He lectured us on public safety, advised us to form neighborhood block groups, and even asked if any of us would wear a wire to expose drug dealers. When someone complained, "Someone threw a brick at me on Alberta Street," he chided her: "You shouldn't ride your bike on Alberta Street." After the meeting in the important evaluation gathering, a key practice in community organizing, leaders were furious: "Why can't we ride our bikes on a public street?" "Would he have given that restriction in a more affluent neighborhood?" "How can we form neighborhood block groups when our neighbors are drug dealers armed with guns?" "We're afraid of these drug houses; we won't put our lives at risk to wear a wire—that's ludicrous."

This was a painful first encounter with a powerful bureaucracy. Later leaders met with a captain who also did nothing, even questioned why "civilians" were trying to tell the police department how to do its job. Getting nowhere led us to the mayor's office. Hearing the particular ins and outs of the drug trafficking in Portland from a large network of ordinary people living in the affected neighborhoods became the first step in developing a strategy of action. Simultaneously, leaders met with city commissioners and the mayor to establish working relationships. Others researched how different cities were responding to this issue across the nation. Soon leaders found a working model in San Diego that was referred to as a drug house ordinance. Here's how it worked:

1. Neighbors call in suspected drug activity to a dedicated drug house hotline at the police bureau.
2. When three or more verifiable reports are received, police research the ownership of the home.
3. Broadly, the ordinance POP sought was a nuisance ordinance, defining drug dealing along with other things as a nuisance-triggering city response.

4. If it is a rental (our research had revealed that 85 percent of drug houses were rentals, often with absentee landlords and rent paid in cash), a letter was sent to the landlord informing them of the drug dealing coming out of the property they owned. They were given a thirty-day period to make a no-cause eviction.

5. If landlords complied, tenants were evicted; if not, a hefty fine could be levied on the landlord.

POP's proposal met stiff resistance from the real estate community, a formidable opposition for this first action. After much back and forth, including testimony from real estate brokers and landlords from POP congregations favoring the ordinance, it was passed. It was a big win and added a new tool to fight crime. It didn't solve the problem, as drug houses often shifted locations swiftly, but it did disrupt the business, and more importantly, it built confidence in the power of ordinary people to make change in their communities. This led us step-by-step into increasingly complex and important issues while honing our skills as public leaders. This was but the beginning for me and for Redeemer in twisting together the strands of spirituality and organizing into a cord of strength and endurance along with other congregational leaders.

> We were now learning by experience what we had been taught in training: no deal is as good as the power it takes to make it stick.

The drug house ordinance passed in May 1987, offering another tool in the fight against drugs in neighborhoods. Then it languished in the backrooms of the largest and most powerful bureaucracy in Portland, the Portland Police Department. We were now learning by experience what we had been taught in training: no deal is as good as the power it takes to make it stick. POP was on the first rung of power, having made a deal. One level of power is to make a deal. It takes more power to keep a deal, because often the promised changes wilt in the implementation stages. To be invited to the table where decisions are made as issues are being framed at the government or market levels is an even higher level of recognition and power.

After the ordinance was passed, local neighborhood leaders steadily reported drug dealing in their neighborhoods with little or no effect. We found out later that the staff and volunteers at the police precinct were keeping records on three-by-five cards with no apparent way to coordinate, update, consolidate, sort, or make sense of reports in order to take action. POP went to work again.

Mayor Bud Clark oversaw the Portland Police Bureau. He was the highest-ranking decision maker, and leaders had already met with him in forging the drug house ordinance. Getting the ordinance passed was only part of the task for POP. Now we had to make sure the ordinance was put into practice. POP organized a large meeting with the mayor. This time the meeting was at Redeemer—in our neighborhood, on our terms, and with our agenda. A couple hundred people packed into Redeemer's basement to confront the mayor and stir him to action on the drug house ordinance.

A local Black-owned newspaper, the *Portland Observer*, blasted headlines on November 25, 1987:

Churches Say City Not Doing Enough

Last Tuesday morning, November 24, 1987, the most talked about subject on Portland television was the meeting that took place at Redeemer Lutheran Church the night before. Organized by the Portland Organizing Project, an alliance of 13 churches from North Portland, Northeast Portland, Northwest Portland and Southeast Portland, the meeting featured Mayor Bud Clark in one corner and citizens from several communities throughout the greater Portland Metropolitan area in the other.[4]

It was a contentious meeting as demands for action were met by excuses from the mayor. For many church members who were

---

[4] "Churches Say City Not Doing Enough," *Portland Observer*, November 25, 1987, front page.

used to being nice, it was a stretch. For others, it was an experience of the world as it is that we needed to change.

In the evaluation period after the meeting, people openly expressed their feelings in a way that recognized others' wholeness, the pros and cons of the meeting were lifted up for affirmation and improvement, and the lessons of power were taught. This important practice of evaluating a meeting right after it occurred, while people were still warm from the experience, became a foundational practice. The pros and cons of the meetings were quickly jotted down for further reflection and action in subsequent meetings.

Leaders, many of whom were performing public action for the first time, were recognized and appreciated. Organizers reiterated lessons of public life: power, negotiations, persistence, preparedness, and the next steps. Over and over again in small and large groups, POP modeled and taught how to exercise power. In my time as pastor of Redeemer, we engaged six Portland mayors and numerous corporate, government, and nonprofit leaders with both firmness and respect—respect we also demanded in return.

HOME AND FAMILY

I fell into God and the world at the same time in the public world of a pastor, with its complex mix of race and class, power and action, prayer and longing. But I also fell into God and the world at the same time within my family. The struggle of our own family mirrored the experience of many in the community and dropped us into a world demanding a more engaged spirituality and a more powerful organizing effort. The bush that burned in the community also burned in our home.

For the time being, things had settled down in the congregation. Our family, on the other hand, struggled. We adopted our second child, a mixed Black and Anglo son, one day after his birth in May 1982. It was the first "child relinquishment" adoption in the state of Oregon, a legal option giving the birth mother the right to choose the adoptive parents by letters submitted to the state. She chose us, and we chose our son.

By his third birthday, however, we were sinking in the swamp of perplexing nurture/nature dynamics. We experienced uncontrollable defiance and aggressive refusals to comply with house rules. Maybe it was normal behavior for a three-year-old. We had to put a lock on our bedroom door. Maybe we were just not capable parents. We called on experts. We leaned on friends to help us. This continued into an adulthood that included residential placements and intensive treatment.

Around the same time, our daughter, eight years old, experienced her first grand mal seizure followed by a painful bout of spinal meningitis that required several excruciating spinal taps. My wife and I accompanied her into the procedure room. The doctor asked me to hold her down while a large needle penetrated her tiny spine. I felt queasy, sweat dripping down my face. I was clammy all over and totally spent when the procedure was done, though we would have to repeat this several times as her illness ran its course. We learned later that our daughter suffered from fetal alcohol effect, a milder form of fetal alcohol syndrome. Fetal alcohol effect manifested in a confusing and nasty array of symptoms that still haunt her: seizures, lack of coordination, impulsivity, judgment deficit. Both children challenged us to our very cores.

In the late 1980s, the heat turned up on us as a couple. We squeezed in time for family counseling. In about the third session, Michelle began to cry. I reached over to give her a box of tissues. She snatched the tissue from the box, almost knocking it out of my hand. The counselor asked to see her alone for the next session.

Soon she enrolled in a twelve-week program at Lutheran Family Services for women who had been sexually abused as children. This experience lay buried in her memory until awakened by the counselor. I learned later that this is not uncommon. I participated in the group for men in relationships with the women going through therapy in their own group. Michelle was angry. She relived horrifying childhood experiences I knew nothing about, nor could I ever as a man really understand. We entered a precarious, thorny phase of our marriage. The kids were needy. We were stricken. Was it us? Were we the source of their troubles? We were flying by the seat of our pants into unknown territory. We were walking a new path, each with rocks in our shoes and our hearts heavy.

Healing came to Michelle in an amazing, graceful manner. When she entered therapy, she saw herself in a dark hole with no escape except to take her own life. As she wrestled with the demons of depression, she plotted how she would kill herself. As therapy took hold, she envisioned herself in a white space just below ground but with high windows. It was a safe, neutral space, like a doctor's office waiting room. Finally, in a miraculous collaboration of her own strong spirit, the power of the women's group, and the mystery of grace, she began to see herself in a broad green meadow with flowers and sunshine. To remember this vision, she changed her legal name to "Greenfield." Her courage, persistence, and gratitude opened her to share this story with the congregation in a wrenching and powerful testimony on a Sunday morning, just as Redeemer was beginning to hear people's stories more deeply.

Meanwhile, financial pressures spiked. I earned a modest salary at Redeemer, and Michelle worked as a licensed practical nurse at Emanuel Hospital, making about as much as I did. However, in the summer of 1986, our mortgage costs reached their apex as we were paying almost $1,000 a month on our $60,000 mortgage. When we bought the house in 1981, the interest rate was 14 percent. We were on a deferred interest plan. Because some of the interest was deferred, the principal didn't budge at all; in fact, it increased. After five years, we still owed almost the total amount we had borrowed. Property values in the neighborhood had also declined, so although the interest rate dipped—though only to 12 percent—banks wouldn't refinance our home because the value of the appraisal had decreased by one-half. Our first home that we purchased for $60,000 was now worth $30,000, and we owed the bank $53,000. The bank suggested we borrow another $20,000 in down payment, then they might renegotiate the loan at 12 percent. What could we do?

PASTOR TERRY TO PASTOR MOE

I chose to go away for a few days on a silent retreat, which was part of our spiritual direction course. I chose a six-day retreat at the Franciscan Renewal Center in Portland. Having never kept my mouth shut for a day, let alone six days in a row, I worried. What would I do? How would the time feel? What if I saw visions or experienced night terrors?

We were asked not to bring books. That would have been a simple way to get through six days of silence, with my nose in a book. Instead, I packed up my briefcase with art supplies: crayons, paints, drawing materials, scissors, glitter, glue, and so on. I stuffed my favorite music cassettes in my suitcase and brought along a small boom box. Having put on this armor to fend off the demons of silence, I checked into my cell and shut my mouth.

Of course, this didn't shut off the chatter in my head and didn't calm the palpitations of my heart. It magnified the one and lasered in on the other. I slept a lot.

Each day I met with a spiritual director for thirty minutes or so, and each evening, we joined in evening prayer. These were the exceptions to the silence rules. No talking with other participants at other times. Meals were silent, as were all the spaces between. For the first three days, I slept sixteen hours a day. Was I really that tired? Was I only avoiding the silence by sleeping? Did my sleepiness mirror a lack of wakefulness in my soul?

My spiritual director kept encouraging me, though, saying, "You can't pray if you're tired." Finally, on the fourth day, I woke up. She noticed it immediately. "Well," she said, "I was wondering when you would join me. I got quite concerned you weren't really going to wake up."

I realized then how dangerously close to disaster I was skating. The really startling thing I came to see is that I didn't know how close to a crisis I was until I stopped. How close to a big fall had I been walking? How near some kind of breakdown had I drifted? I recognized how I might have slogged right into a heart attack or slid into risky behavior, as I had seen others do. Who knows what might have happened had this intervention not come? In my room, I drew a diagram with a crack through the middle, with my old self on one side of the page and my new self, really not yet emerging but having been glimpsed, on the other. Here is that diagram:[5]

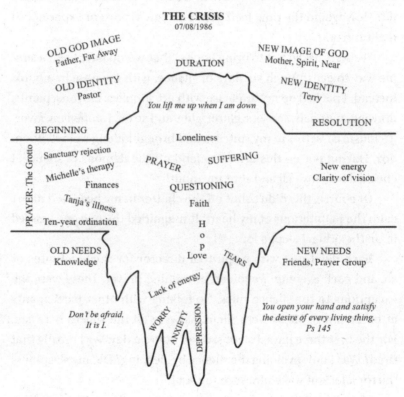

FIGURE 3.1. The crisis

With my silent retreat experience whirling in my head and heart, I returned to our family and congregation. I, too, decided to change my name, at least the way I preferred to be addressed by the congregation, from Pastor Terry to Pastor Moe. Some applauded this

---

[5] Personal journal, July 8, 1986.

as a way for me to claim the authority of the pastor's office, as they had been used to in previous decades. For me, however, it arose out of my crisis: I needed to protect my baptismal name and encourage a distinction between my personal and pastoral identities. Later on, in a ten-day organizing training, I learned about the tension of negotiating public-private roles and identities. It is a notion that has served me well and that I still struggle to apply. This shift proved to be a pivotal shift for me and the congregation going forward, a kind of break with what was and an openness to something different. At home, things were changing as well.

> I, too, decided to change my name, at least the way I preferred to be addressed by the congregation, from Pastor Terry to Pastor Moe.

While I was on my silent retreat, my newly energized and resilient wife put down earnest money on a new house. "Well, I only put down $500 in earnest money and signed some papers," she explained. "We can still get out of it if you want—we just lose the $500. I hope you like the house," she concluded. What was I to say?

I liked the house. It was just three blocks from where we were living, which had a strangling mortgage that suspended us in limbo. Anita and Gerry were a mixed-race family, and their children were close to the ages of ours. They lived near our old house in the neighborhood, and somehow Michelle and Anita met when they agreed to carpool together to zoo camp for our son and their daughter. Over the week, they became fast friends. Michelle must have shared our housing dilemma, because while I was away, with my head in the sounds of silence, Anita invited Michelle to look at the house next to hers. It was for sale for $45,000: a gorgeous craftsman home built in 1913, with hardwood floors, three full bedrooms, and two baths. But how could we ever slash our way through the cords of debt that held us captive? How could we afford another down payment? And the bank interest rate was still 12 percent.

The answer emerged as miraculously as the story of the paralyzed man lowered to Jesus through the roof of a house by his friends,[6] a kind of desperate, frantic effort coupled with the grace of God. What I later learned from Black matriarchs—"God makes a way where there ain't no way"—now applied to us. The solution presented to us was an amalgamation of two critical parts that had to line up in sequence in a short window: a blind assumption of the seller's mortgage and a surrender of our current mortgage to the bank in lieu of foreclosure. What?

First the seller had to agree to let us assume their mortgage. Basically, they signed over their mortgage to us at the interest rate they were paying, which was 8 percent. The sellers were a young couple, both teachers, who were moving to California. It was already July, so they were eager to leave, and the selling market was very poor. They asked $45,000. We signed the papers and assumed their interest rate on the $45,000. The other part was more complicated. Our realtor had explained that the bank would not foreclose if we voluntarily turned over our deed "in lieu of foreclosure," she called it. We would lose all the equity in our home, which at this point was negative, even though we had paid over $50,000 in monthly payments in the five-plus years we lived there. We signed the papers, made the deal, and moved three blocks away to a larger, more desirable home still less than a mile from Redeemer. Like the crowd's reaction to Jesus's mighty deeds, we were astonished, amazed, and perplexed.

It wasn't all roses, however. One negative was that our credit was damaged. Though we never saw any formal repercussions from our "in lieu of foreclosure" deal, our applications for credit cards were denied for the next seven years. In a way, maybe that was a good thing. A more profound shadow side lay in the fact that we were one of thousands caught in the economic turbulence of the early 1980s: during the recession in 1983, high inflation and unemployment resulted in many foreclosures. We had escaped, but many did not. We refinanced several times over the coming years, made

---

[6] Mark 2:1–12.

improvements to the home, and when we finally moved away in 2012, sold the house for over $400,000. This time, the equity was positive. Enough to purchase our more modest home in Portland's first suburban ring, a ranch home valued at $250,000. Later, this personal experience with housing influenced me, as through organizing, we developed a campaign for affordable housing.

MEANWHILE AT REDEEMER

All this pressure in our family and blossoming spirituality in me met both welcome and caution flags at Redeemer. We became good family friends with another young couple from church, Lonnie and Nancy Phelps and their children. We hung out with them on weekends, shared meals in the winter, and picnicked at a riverfront park followed by lunch at Sunshine Pizza in the summer. Though skirting the line of public/private, pastor/friend, the Phelpses became close and remain so to this day.

At church, I discovered members who were also into prayer and spirituality in various forms. Some were well past my introductory stage. My closest friend and soon-to-be colleague in both prayer and organizing, Nancy Phelps, had already been in a weekly prayer group for many years. Together we formed the Health Care Cabinet to visit and pray with others as well as to offer groups and classes at Redeemer. We instigated a spiritual phase in the life of Redeemer. We introduced guided meditation into worship. I included new spiritual insights in my sermons. Clearly, we were still the early adopters, but soon more people got comfortable, and most at least tolerated our experiments.

> We instigated a spiritual phase in the life of Redeemer. We introduced guided meditation into worship.

Eventually we offered a healing prayer after Sunday worship about once a month. When only a few people came, we decided to incorporate a period for healing prayer within the Sunday liturgy. This included a quiet meditation with music, a station for prayer with the laying of hands, and a station for anointing at the baptismal font. We instituted these healing services in the Sunday liturgy on the fifth Sunday every month and whenever the lessons indicated healing. Some in the pews were very uncomfortable. Others, especially the children, embraced it.

The night before our first healing service in Sunday worship, I had a dream. I was driving a big truck, like a moving van or garbage truck, on a narrow, winding road. I was in the cab but not used to driving a top-heavy truck. As the road got steeper, the truck lurched forward faster and faster. I struggled to keep on the road. Finally, the truck and I flew off a ledge, and I was thrown from the cab, only to find myself impaled on a deer's antlers. Clearly this was an anxiety dream! Psychologizing aside, I was living the tension of our first healing service. It came off fine for the first time, and we made adjustments over the years. This first public healing service during the regular worship hour made space for other shifts in worship and proved a critical step in our congregational development.

I recall our daughter coming forward to sit in the prayer chair while members prayed with and for her. Her tiny legs dangled, not touching the floor. Her life also dangled precipitously on the edge, though we only had a foreshadowing of what was to come. When she was five, she accompanied me in a street march with the Black United Front. We paused in front of a smutty movie theater and shouted, "Shut it down! Shut it down!" before moving to the other chants and issues. One day later on, she would come to face many of the issues we were protesting: sexual violence, racism, drugs, and gangs. But the street we marched down did change, and that march became enshrined in her memory. Years later, something would remind her, and she would say, "Dad, remember when we shut that porn theater down?" "Yes, I do," I replied. And soon these protests moved to a place within a larger strategy called community organizing.

One of the critical shifts in Redeemer's culture was to expand beyond the one-hour, self-imposed time limit on Sunday mornings.

A large clock in the back of the sanctuary was clearly visible from the pulpit and altar, a constant reminder of the "sacred hour" we were trespassing. Some in the congregation checked their watches in obvious gestures, and the length of the services was a source of debate at coffee hour and council meetings. We persisted in the healing services periodically as we gradually created more space for spirituality within the Lutheran framework.

If the dance within the congregation was an awkward one step forward / two steps back, the community opened a new and exciting dance floor with many moving parts. My instinct was to engage the community in some kind of social ministry. My reading of liberation theology in seminary and in my first parish (1976–81) brought with it a hunger for engagement. My denomination offered a fantastic opportunity in a series of social ministry conferences that were decades ahead of the curve:

1. Systems Change Conference, March 6–11, 1986, Miami, FL
2. Coalition Building Conference, February 26–March 3, 1987, Miami, FL
3. Strategic Planning Conference, March 23–29, 1988, Miami, FL

Through these conferences, my instincts were affirmed, and my views broadened. It was at these conferences over three years that I first encountered a mature community-organizing effort with a list of accomplishments. People United to Lead the Struggle for Equality Inc. (PULSE) grew out of the race riots in 1980 in Miami. Meeting the leaders and hearing their stories confirmed my growing interest in what was brewing in Portland and would eventually become POP.

I was aware I was changing. I was being transformed. Something precious and irrevocable was being given in this precarious, crazy time. We were becoming more ourselves, more whole, more open, more real. The fire that burns and is not consumed was inviting us to pay attention. As I turned to the burning bush of the community, the congregation also began to reach out, first to the children. Through a bustling vacation church school, hundreds of neighborhood children sang and prayed and jostled their way around a holy center. Gradually, children began to come for Sunday school and worship. The number coming forward for the children's message burgeoned from two or three to fifteen or twenty.

RAINBOWS IN THE STORMS

October 10, 1988, was the happiest day of my thirty-two-year ministry. On this day, the heavens opened, and I glimpsed a rainbow church falling from the clouds and landing in our community in the form of a mass baptism. I was the proudest pastor in the world. More importantly, I was beginning to see the potential of a multicultural congregation, a dream I safe-harbored in the depths of my heart.

> We were becoming more ourselves, more whole, more open, more real. The fire that burns and is not consumed was inviting us to pay attention.

On that day, nineteen young people crowded into the gathering space of Redeemer, the old sanctuary now cleared out to make way for a whole new church to enter. Here children of every race and color—at least it seemed so to us—came to the waters of baptism in a single rainbow service. Red, yellow, Black, brown, and white, they came. Refugee children from Laos claimed their heavenly citizenship. Grandchildren and great-grandchildren of Black elders of the church who once could not eat in restaurants in Portland now generations later pressed forward to receive the free gift of grace. New mixed-race children from the neighborhood straggled in with their single parents, uncles or aunts, or grandparents. Among the throng were two Native American children, the Two-Twos (because their last name was Two-Two), young children of the Pine Ridge Reservation born in poverty and addiction. Whole families, parts of larger clans, came eagerly to the font.

"You are baptized in the name of the Father, and of the Son, and of the Holy Spirit," I repeated nineteen times, as the congregation resounded each time, "Amen! And Amen!" Then each family anointed their children, "You have been sealed by the Holy Spirit and marked by the cross of Christ forever." And "Amens" rang from every corner of the room.

Like the Holy Wind wending over the waters, that day was chaos—and it was a new creation. Too many people crowded into the space. Not everyone could hear. Babies and children were passed through the crowd to the font and then back again as blessings were given and candles distributed. Parents and grandparents joined the congregation as the Gospel was read in Lao and English: "Let the children come, and do not hinder them." No sermon was necessary.

> Here children of every race and color—at least it seemed so to us—came to the waters of baptism in a single rainbow service.

When the Saleumvong family, Laotian refugees, came forward, I saw their sponsors, two white elders who had met them at the airport, helped them find a house to rent, and brought them food and groceries—and more importantly, who had learned to eat their food and to love their children. Rainbow energy filled the room. We were filled with the Holy Spirit, all of us. It was my proudest moment. I felt as though God's kingdom had come, and we were part of it. It was among the greatest days of my life. I'll never forget it.

As often is the case, rainbows appear in the wake of storms. Already more young Black men had been killed by gunfire in our neighborhood over the summer than ever before, seventy-seven in all. Abandoned houses became havens for gangs and drugs. Bullet holes pierced the stained glass of our sanctuary windows that faced the school across the street. Those precious in God's sight were vulnerable to a hostile world outside. Our family and congregation fell precipitously and helplessly off the edge of some kind of normalcy into a gaping chasm of uncertainty.

Our own daughter, our precious Tanja, just twelve years old, who came to the healing service to be touched by God, ran away. I was white, working class, male, and educated and had all the privileges of middle-class American status. I realized my life was wedded on the one hand to power and privilege. At the same time, I was being immersed in my family and in my church community in a world of vulnerability, violence, and powerlessness. Redeemer would continue to struggle with its role in the two worlds it, too, inhabited. Meanwhile, the rainbow day in October 1988 resounded and begged for more.

Rev. Kelly Chatman, a Black Lutheran pastor from Detroit, was called by a neighboring congregation and, along with his wife, Cheryl, began many ministries under the umbrella of Peer Support Ministries. Cheryl and a sixteen-year-old Black woman, Kim Robinson, who worked in the childcare center in the basement of Redeemer, began a children's choir: the Hallelujah Kids. Women of the congregation sewed colorful dashiki stoles that easily slipped over their heads and shone with the bright patterns of their heritage. Soon Saturday-afternoon practices and Sunday-morning performances were rocking Redeemer and other congregations nearby as the Hallelujah Kids swayed and clapped on the offbeat to boisterous piano accompaniment:

I will call upon the Lord, who is worthy to be praised:
so shall I be saved from mine enemies.
The Lord liveth; and blessed be my rock;
and let the God of my salvation be exalted.[7]

One summer, they traveled to Holden Village, a Lutheran retreat center six hours from Portland in the North Cascades Mountains. Another time they traveled to Eastern Oregon to perform at small rural congregations there. The sweet rainbow of prophetic longing

[7] From their title song based on Psalm 18.

and our dreams seemed near at hand. The voices of these young people seemed to rise above the chaotic waters of their neighborhood. Their spirit was strong.

Looking back, it seems the window of this rainbow promise opened and closed so quickly. It opened oh so briefly, like an angel in a dream, and then slammed shut, leaving us breathlessly behind to ponder. Perched around these vulnerable children, however, like the great dragon in Revelation 12, forces threatened to devour this new offspring of the rainbow. Perhaps it has never been any different in the history of the struggle. Like Moses thrust into the Nile in a basket, these children, and our own adopted children, were adrift in a world twisted and torn by oppression, racism, violence, and inequity.

The congregation, too, began to realize its own Egyptian and Hebrew mix. The cultural shell that formed Redeemer in the 1950s and 1960s now struggled to break free. Like a kind of prison, the windows of the church obscured by rose, emerald, and indigo cuts of glass not only prevented people from seeing the world outside, but blocked those outside from seeing inside our community. In 2007, when the narthex windows were finally replaced with clear glass, an elder remarked, "We put those opaque windows in so people couldn't see in." We were turning a corner, though, and eventually the culture of the congregation shifted. Retreats that once had been experienced as laborious planning just to hold our heads above water now turned into real retreats, oases of rest, reflection, prayer, and community.

At the end of the 1980s, I had completed an apprenticeship in spirituality and organizing. I completed the two-year practicum in spiritual direction, was elected president of POP, and began to walk more deeply on the holy ground near the bush that still burns. Many in the congregation didn't understand the mystery we were encountering. Nor did I, to tell the truth. But many also yearned for what was coming, knowing only by feel how the steps were fitting together. Somehow together, we walked on holy ground, making a commitment to be a teaching parish for seminary interns, but first I negotiated a three-month sabbatical for the summer of 1990.

FOR REFLECTION

This chapter includes a messy mix of organizing, family, and congregational wrestling.

- What is your experience with the "messy mix" of personal and public?

The story of the nineteen baptisms, the "rainbow church," was a highlight of ministry for Pastor Moe and Redeemer.

- What have been your most satisfying experiences?
- How have they impacted you and others?

Part **2**

WALKING ON
HOLY GROUND

1991–2000

4 REMOVING OUR SANDALS

When the Lord saw that he had turned aside to look, God called to him out of the bush: "Moses! Moses!" He answered, "Here I am." And He said, "Do not come closer. Remove your sandals from your feet, for the place on which you stand is holy ground."[1]

—Exodus 3:4–5

[The word] Ecstasy comes from the Greek "ek stasis" and implies moving out of stasis, out of a set position. Of course, the word is used for spiritual transport, but it strikes me that the church ought to see its daily role as following a path of ecstasy, leaving behind all that is stagnant and staid and stepping out into the unknown, allowing ourselves to be displaced as we enter into relationship with others in their space.[2]

—Heidi Neumark

We need the harsh candor of a poet like Hafiz. "Love wants to reach out and manhandle us," he says, "breaking all our teacup talk of God.... It wants to drag you by the hair and rip from your grip all the toys of the world that bring you no joy."[3]

—Belden C. Lane

SABBATICAL: SUMMER 1990

I PLANNED MY SABBATICAL WITH A COMMITTEE TO HELP ME CLARIFY THE process and to communicate with the congregation. I consulted with Oregon Synod staff, met with colleagues who had made sabbaticals,

[1] Exodus 3:4–5, JPS H-ET.
[2] Heidi Neumark, *Breathing Space: A Spiritual Journey in the South Bronx* (Boston: Beacon, 2003), 32.
[3] Belden C. Lane, *Backpacking with the Saints: Wilderness Hiking as Spiritual Practice* (New York: Oxford University Press, 2015), 34.

read a couple of books on sabbaticals from the Alban Institute, and then put together a plan in four segments:

1. *First two weeks: home and family.* A time to stay home every day and not go to Redeemer. Time to work on the yard and build a deck I wanted to get to before summer.
2. *Next five weeks: deroling.* A time to work in the "real world" in order to earn money for my thirty-day retreat and to experience the workaday world. I worked for Labor Force, "Daily Work for Daily Pay." I would go into the office at 6:30 a.m., would be sent out on a job, and then would return at about 4:30 p.m. I earned $35 a day on my assignment at Ivy Hi-Lift, where I sorted, stacked, loaded, and unloaded scaffolding ladders, ropes, cables, and other kinds of equipment for painters, construction workers, and builders.
3. *Core of the sabbatical: thirty-day retreat.* While I had set aside resources to go anywhere for this longed-for experience, I settled on the "Prayer of the Heart" retreat at Shalom Prayer Center in Mount Angel, where my spiritual director, Sister Antoinette, was the retreat guide.
4. *Final two weeks: home and family.* Similar to the first two weeks.

I leaned forward into my hard-earned sabbatical, cherishing every day in the new freedom. By the end of the first seven weeks of sabbatical, I was ready for the heart of it, the thirty-day retreat. Deciding to spend the time at Mount Angel with Sister Antoinette as my director was the right discernment.

"PRAYER OF THE HEART," SHALOM PRAYER
CENTER, MOUNT ANGEL, OREGON

July 2–July 31, 1990

The "Prayer of the Heart" brochure said, "The focus of this month-long experience will be the centering prayer method and the dynamic transformation that is initiated by resting in the Lord." I was not disappointed. When I first stepped onto the retreat grounds on July 2, 1990, summer rains had cleared the air, and the sun shone brightly through wafting clouds as if to welcome me. As I walked to my room to get settled, head in the clouds, I stepped ankle-deep into a large mud puddle, soaking my tennis shoe and the hem of my jeans. What? A sign of welcome? A warning to stay grounded? This was the auspicious beginning of a life-changing adventure.

I reflected back on this experience years later: "Taking time for prayer and reflection in such an intentional way drove me deeper into the cave of prayer and organizing where the shadows of the present dance in dim light between hope and despair. Striking a match and building a small fire in the cave's entrails, I approached my grief and reckoned with my future."[4]

I immersed myself in the solitude and silence of this precious sabbatical gift. When the group went on to watch videos on centering prayer, I asked to be excused to walk more along the creek, to be still, to let my soul catch up with the awful grief within me, especially the pain of our daughter running away and being on the street. As I prayed in a chair in the orchard next to the cemetery, I longed for peace and serenity. On the twenty-eighth day of the retreat, just days before its ending, I settled in a great peace, a peace that passes human understanding, a peace I knew was there all along and could be accessed anytime, anywhere.

I wasn't done with grief and prayer, but I was ready to go on.

---

[4] Terry Allen Moe, "O Healing River: Just Prayer and Organizing" (DMin thesis, Wesley Theological Seminary, 1998), 15.

REDEEMER BECOMES A TEACHING PARISH FOR SEMINARY INTERNS

Leaders at Redeemer had dreamed of becoming an internship site
before I came on as pastor, but this dream was lost in the abrupt
pastoral transition. A close POP colleague, Rev. Harold Kurtz of Ken-
ton Ave. Presbyterian, encouraged me to contact a friend of his in
the Contextual Education Department at Luther Seminary in Saint
Paul, Minnesota. Harold and his friend Denny Everson had been mis-
sionaries together in Ethiopia in the Mekane Jesus (House of Jesus)
Church, a joint Presbyterian/Lutheran outreach there.

Harold and I had been designated to knock on the door of the
Housing Authority of Portland (HAP) during the drug house campaign. Though a public agency, HAP meetings were private with no
seeming accountability. Correspondence and phone calls were not
answered, so Harold and I, bedecked in our collars, were sent to its
office. HAP's executive director was a former sheriff and a powerful,
connected part of the establishment. Harold took the lead. He spoke
clearly and with persistence when someone answered the door, but
she refused to let us in. Harold had been a pilot in World War II,
had been a missionary in Ethiopia, and was a well-respected pastor
and leader. Still the door remained shut. We learned to turn this no
into even more aggressive action, eventually getting the attention of
the mayor and several commissioners. I learned a lot from Harold
and missed him dearly when he took a national position with the
Presbyterian Church. As I ponder the role of organizing, the capacity
to hold others accountable to community values rises to the top of
priorities, difficult as it is to pull off.

Though Harold and I couldn't crack the door of HAP, his creden-
tialing of me with Denny Everson at the seminary was golden. This
was yet another example of the many ways the relational network
of organizing impacted me and once again proved the truism "It's
all about relationships!" Redeemer applied to be a teaching parish
in the ELCA through the Horizon program, a funding partnership
that opened opportunities for urban, multicultural, and rural congregations to have interns even when the congregation couldn't

afford it on their own. It made sense to have future pastors trained in a variety of settings, and not only in affluent congregations that could afford them.

I never wanted the lack of funding to be a reason not to begin new initiatives. The commitment to not let money get in the way of vision was a challenging pledge, but over the years, it stretched our vision, taught us tenacity, and increased our capacity overall to take on bigger challenges.

> I never wanted the lack of funding to be a reason not to begin new initiatives.

We were accepted. Horizon brokered a three-way funding deal for the internship: one-third would come from national resources, one-third from the synod, and one-third from the congregation. This made it feasible for Redeemer to become a teaching parish in the ELCA, even though we had to reach out to local congregations and grants for additional support that the Oregon Synod couldn't offer. This proved to be valuable learning. Our first of nineteen interns, Sue Selffert, arrived in December 1990, just after my reentry to Redeemer after my sabbatical.

Because Horizon worked with all eight Lutheran seminaries for placement of interns, Redeemer benefited from fresh perspectives and cultures from different geographic areas: North Carolina, Maryland, New England, Minnesota, and California. Additionally, it connected me over the years with seven of the eight seminaries of our church, though most of our interns came from Luther and my alma mater, Pacific Lutheran Theological Seminary (PLTS) in Berkeley.

I cannot overemphasize how these pastors-to-be, mostly women (fourteen of nineteen), impacted me and the congregation. Becoming a teaching parish bolstered Redeemer. I learned how to supervise and mentor these interns, a practice that unfolded in Transformational Leadership after leaving Redeemer. We learned from each other and grew in our understanding of church as a whole. Our first interns were all women. This was good for Redeemer and me. They taught us how women can lead and change the church. Our second intern,

Jacqueline Moren, encouraged us to use inclusive language. We made many changes in Sunday liturgy, though the official books we used were still difficult to negotiate. She suggested that we look at how to change the language of the baptismal rite: "I baptize you in the name of the Father, and of the Son, and of the Holy Spirit. Amen." I was hesitant to mess with this ancient formula. We worked on two changes, however. First, we changed "I baptize you" to "You are baptized." Then rather than changing the ancient formula itself, we added a phrase on the end: "You are baptized in the name of the Father, and of the Son, and of the Holy Spirit, *one God, Mother of us all*" (emphasis mine). It was one of many shifts that interns brought over the years.

I am so grateful for the interns who brought their gifts and perspectives to Redeemer. Frankly, my motive was as much about organizing as it was about Redeemer. By 1990, I was a primary leader in POP and had grown to see organizing as a key element in congregational mission. I began to think strategically about our synod and denomination. Could organizing revitalize our congregations, which even in the 1990s were beginning to shrivel? I wanted other pastors to have a taste of the power of organizing, and what better way than to invite future pastors to spend a year in an organizing congregation?

> Redeemer was awakening from its drowsy middle-class malaise to a role in God's work for justice.

As Moses was confronted by the burning bush and called out of his Egyptian upbringing to become the liberator of the Hebrew people, so Redeemer was awakening from its drowsy middle-class malaise to a role in God's work for justice.

We weren't quite an organizing congregation, but we were engaged in learning the arts and practices and mindset of organizing while connecting deeply into the relational network of leadership and institutions that build power. Together with our interns, other congregations, colleagues, and organizers, we developed a relational culture of power. It was a steep learning curve in the early 1990s, one that would impact Redeemer as we confronted some of the painful issues of the community and opened us internally to our frailty as a congregation. We were walking barefoot on holy ground.

From shutting down drug houses and cleaning up illegal dumpsites in the late 1980s, POP organized around several larger issues in the early 1990s, including affordable housing.

POP HOLDS A PRESS CONFERENCE IN THE LOBBY OF A LOCAL BANK

Pastor John Rodgers, my close colleague from Vernon Presbyterian just seven blocks east of Redeemer, stood in the lobby of Security Pacific Bank in downtown Portland by a large map of bank investments in neighborhoods. This map displayed the disparity between deposits and returns to certain neighborhoods. This was redlining thinly cloaked. We had not asked permission to do a press conference in the lobby of a local bank, but by the time security knew what was happening, the TV cameras were rolling. My job, dressed in my clericals, was to intercept security while the press conference continued. POP addressed many issues in the early nineties, sometimes confronting decision makers as in the example above, as well as doing necessary research and background relational work to make actions effective:

- *Homeownership.* In three years of organizing, POP successfully leveraged Portland's largest banks to commit tens of millions of dollars of new investment for Portland's poorer communities. Project leaders used federal legislation, the Community Reinvestment Act, passed in 1972, to leverage these banks. It wasn't easy. We had asked for meetings with bank presidents, only to be rebuffed. One president sat behind his desk with his feet up on the desk, leaning back leisurely while we tried to share our concerns with him. When leaders set up a press conference in the lobby of one of these banks with TV cameras rolling, we got a productive meeting with bank presidents the next day. Soon major banks opened community loan offices in blighted neighborhoods.

- *Fred Meyer store remodeling.* POP leaders worked to keep a North Portland major grocery store open. Often poorer neighborhoods became food deserts, and access to fresh and healthy food required traveling long distances. Already a Fred Meyer store near Redeemer the Walnut Park branch, had closed, leaving a boarded-up building on a major intersection. The North Interstate store seemed to be next in line for closure. This store was located at an important cross street with four bus lines and was a lifeline for many working-class folks who shopped there. Members of North Portland congregations, including our sister congregation, Bethel Lutheran, noticed that things didn't look right at their store. The building was looking shoddy. The painted lines in the parking lot were fading. Store shelves began to look sparser. Working up the chain of command from the local manager to the president of Fred Meyer Corporation, POP succeeded in getting Fred Meyer to invest $2 million to remodel this 70,000-square-foot store, bringing not only much-needed services to the neighborhood but also forty-five new jobs. We were acting on one of the key principles of organizing: get to the highest-ranking decision maker you can to negotiate for what is needed.

- *Cutting sewer costs.* An opportunity came to engage new and existing congregations in the first-ring suburbs of Southeast and Northeast Portland when the City of Portland was mandated by state and federal environmental entities to clean up the Willamette River by fixing its one-hundred-year-old combined sewer overflow system. Most days this worked well, but seven to ten days a year, the system would become overwhelmed by rainwater dumping raw sewage into the Willamette River. The city's answer to the mandate: make bigger pipes and pass the cost on to homeowners. While no evidence existed that pollution was coming from cesspools or septic tanks, citizens were required to connect to the main Portland sewer system in the single largest public works project in the country, all at the expense of local homeowners. It was a boondoggle for local plumbers and contractors, most of whom were honest and upstanding, but the creation of this new demand increased opportunities for unscrupulous and predatory contractors to thrive. Many angry residents of East Portland vocally opposed the whole project. Like many protest efforts, this one was fated to end without results. Organizing leaders, including Nancy Phelps from Redeemer, whose home was being assessed for the project, took a more pragmatic approach. What might be accomplished to reduce the impact on homeowners, many of whom were facing sewer assessment costs of $8,000–$10,000, up to one-fourth of the value of many of the homes in the neighborhood? After initial negotiations with city officials, POP organized two large public meetings at two different parishes in Northeast and Southeast Portland. At each meeting, 700 to 750 citizens turned out as members of congregations and others reached out in their neighborhoods. These meetings negotiated an agreement with Earl Blumenauer, the commissioner in charge of the Bureau of Environmental Services. The agreement created a safety net for low-income households; it reduced the average sewer assessment by $2,500 or more by speeding up the project by several years, thus saving millions in interest. Most importantly, it demonstrated the power of collective action. Ordinary people can act effectively in the public realm. Hot anger can lead to useless protest. Organizing is activism that makes sense.[5]

- *Making a big difference.* Leaders estimated that POP had made an impact on the city of over $100 million on these three issues in a single year. Congregations together can make a big difference, a difference well beyond what their local budgets might indicate. This was power leveraged for the common good.
- *Developing leaders.* At the same time, POP was developing strong leaders who worked alongside leaders from other congregations.

---

[5] Gregory F. Augustine Pierce, *Activism That Makes Sense: Congregations and Community Organization* (Chicago: ACTA, 1997). Greg was an early organizer in IAF and remains a leader in Chicago. This was one of the first books recommended by Kevin Jeans-Gail and Mike Miller in their presentations to leaders in Portland early on.

These leaders also began to use their newly gained savvy to help strengthen their own parishes.

One Sunday, we recognized Nancy Phelps's leadership in the sewer campaign; we put a crown on her head, placed over her shoulders a bright-red sash, and named her the "POP Sewer Queen." She, the mother of three, would later reflect how the eighteen months of this campaign were like two terms of pregnancy, each with ups and downs, nausea, and labor to make it to the end.

These were a few of the important hands-on actions that I and Redeemer members joined. We were learning the power of organized people in the public realm. At the same time, we were seeing how organizing could impact our congregational life. Spirituality and organizing were not separate realms but were coming together.

DEEPER INTO ORGANIZING THROUGH IAF

As important as the issues were, Redeemer was embracing the relational work of building community internally as well. Soon leaders of Redeemer were organizing house meetings and conversations about issues both inside the congregation and in the neighborhood. Leaders reached out to neighbors not only to "come to church," but to act on their interests in the community. Further training and focus came to POP and our congregations in 1992, when POP officially became an affiliate of the IAF, the oldest and largest community-organizing network in the US, tracing its lineage back to Saul Alinsky and the backyards of Chicago in the 1940s.[6]

> Redeemer was embracing the relational work of building community internally as well.

---

[6] See the excellent book by Miller and Schutz, eds., *People Power*.

In July 1992, I participated in the IAF ten-day leadership training in Los Angeles, what my colleague Father Jack Mosbrucker later described as "the most effective and helpful continuing education I have ever experienced." I was among the first to attend the IAF national training from Portland, and over the next few years, many priests, pastors, and lay leaders participated, including Nancy Phelps, Redeemer's "Sewer Queen," who later was called to work for POP as an organizer and would grow into a strong and influential leader in the congregation. She played a strategic role in the transformation of Redeemer to Leaven / Salt and Light and continues as a leader in the Leaven community to this day.

In early July 1992, I arrived at Mount St. Mary's College, high above the Pacific in Brentwood, an elite suburb of Los Angeles situated across a rugged crevice from Michael Jackson's Neverland home, for the IAF ten-day leadership training. Why were we here? Why were we on the mountain and not down in the valley where the action was? After all, the Rodney King riots had just devastated South Central Los Angeles (now named South Los Angeles) in May of that year. South Central was still smoking—both literally and figuratively—following the release of the six Los Angeles police officers who brutally beat Rodney King, a Black citizen, the latest in a string of police brutality cases in Los Angeles. I had witnessed similar incidents in Portland, including the case of Tony Stevenson, who was killed by a white police officer using a choke hold on April 21, 1985, as cited earlier. The violence would continue in Portland and other cities throughout the country despite protests and a string of ineffective citizen committees instituted to audit police. As of August 2020, this is still an issue, being reworked once again in Portland as a result of the murder of George Floyd in Minneapolis in May 2020.

The conference did take us to South Central, but only after significant teaching and interaction with sixty clergy, rabbis, union organizers, teachers, principals, health care professionals, and other community leaders from all over the country.

Among the many profound and helpful insights for me was the teaching on three of the key concepts of organizing: individual meetings; how leadership demands attention to the public and private dimensions of our lives, called public/private in the training; and mediating institutions. I now clearly identify the individual meeting—the one-to-one or the relational meeting, as it is now named—as the single most important and life-changing organizing practice.[7]

Conference participants spent a whole day—more than on any other content piece—on the individual meeting or one-to-one. Mike Gecan of Metro IAF writes, "An individual meeting is a face-to-face, one-to-one meeting, in someone's home or apartment or workplace or local coffee shop that takes about 30 minutes. The purpose of the meeting is not chitchat, whining, selling, gossip, sports talk, data collection, or therapy. The aim of the meeting is to initiate a public relationship with another person."[8]

> I now clearly identify the individual meeting—the one-to-one or the relational meeting, as it is now named—as the single most important and life-changing organizing practice.

After the trainer and a participant modeled a one-to-one in front of the group, the trainer debriefed the meeting, pointing out the places of agitation, weak responses, stories that added to the conversation, and questions that helped or hindered the conversation. Then they explained the practice of one-to-ones, what they are and what they are not. Following that, everybody paired up for one-to-ones right in the room, followed by small group one-to-ones in which each person made an individual meeting with another in front of the small group, followed by specific feedback from the trainer and participants. It was rigorous, intense, and impactful. For me, it not only has become part of my organizing art

---

[7] See appendix 1 for more on one-to-ones.
[8] Michael Gecan, *Effective Organizing for Congregational Renewal* (Skokie, IL: ACTA, 2008), 7.

but has a prominent place in my rule of life, the spiritual practices I follow regularly.

In 1998, I committed myself to a discipline of ten relational meetings each week for the duration of Lent. When Easter came, I was so moved by the life-giving experience of these meetings that I continued the commitment through the rest of my ministry at Redeemer.

The teaching on public/private impacted me as well. As I grew as a professional pastor and leader, I was learning that some things were private or personal and others were public, but this session proposed that we live in a tension between the two. Lives lived totally in one or the other sphere miss out on the fullness or abundance of life available. One issue discussed was the importance of dressing for power. This caught my attention, especially since I was emulating the Black pastors I so admired in the Albina Ministerial Alliance, most of whom dressed to the nines. I dressed in sharp three-piece suits with dress shirts and colorful ties. Jerry Garcia ties became my favorites. This was a shift for me, as I hadn't thought much about dressing for power. I learned that dressing up helped me focus on my role representing the people in the congregation and helped me be aware of presenting myself in a respectful and strong manner. I had been content with jeans and a work shirt. I learned in organizing to dress for power instead.

I thought about my dad, who as a working man took his shower after work when he got home, his work clothes hung up for the next day. He wore a suit on Sundays when we went to church. In contrast, I showered and shaved in the morning and put on my Sunday best for each workday and changed into regular clothes on weekends or evenings, if I was off.

Clothing was only one factor. We learned about public roles. Our trainers taught, "We don't call officials by their first names but 'Mr. Mayor' or 'Commissioner So-and-So.' We aren't palsy-walsy with public officials or corporate leaders who are decision makers. We hold them accountable to the offices they hold." I thought of when I asked the congregation to address me as "Pastor Moe" or "Terry." After a while, even my closest friends in the congregation called me

"Pastor Moe" in public, though in private. I was always "Terry." I wasn't a pastor all the time, and that was a relief. At the same time, the insights of public/private helped me maintain a focus and accountability to the many roles I played. My collar wasn't just a God thing. It was a world thing as well. That's why when Redeemer members would see me in my clericals, they would say, "Pastor! Are you leading a service or going to city hall?" Spirituality and organizing were blending in the collar I wore, in my heart for compassion and justice, and in the congregation I was serving, which was now awakening to a new role in society.

I also learned the meaning and importance of mediating institutions at the conference. Mediating institutions do the following:

- buffer and protect individuals and families from the harsh impacts of the larger culture
- offer a lens to interpret experience apart from powerful media messages or propaganda
- make space to form and develop values based on traditions of democracy and religion
- form a sturdy platform for action in the larger arenas of society

The teaching on mediating institutions agitated me. Was Redeemer a mediating institution? Did it protect, help interpret, form faith values of, and launch action for the common good? Did other congregations in my circle see themselves and act as mediating institutions? "Yes and no" was my answer. We had work to do.

During this time, Kevin Jeans-Gail chose to leave POP in order to better take care of his family, now grown to three children. He took a job with a brick company to make more money. Later, when his friend Jim Francesconi ran for city council, Kevin became his chief of staff. It was interesting to have our former organizer on the other side of the table in negotiations. His successor, Kathy Turner, grew POP to eighteen congregations and was the organizer behind the big actions outlined earlier, particularly the sewer issue. She also instigated POP's move from an independent community-organizing entity to becoming a member of the IAF network for the sake of training, credibility, staff support, and funding recognition.

ORGANIZING SPIRITUALITY INSIDE REDEEMER

Candle Prayers, Prayer Circles, and Retreats

Intern Solveig Nilsen-Goodin, 1994–95, introduced Redeemer to "candle prayers," a very simple and profound way to invite deeper and more heartfelt participation in public prayer without adding too much stress for shy Lutherans. Over time, many variations of this practice took shape at Redeemer, but the most common form was to invite people to step forward to a station containing votives or small tapers, light them from a common flame, and place them on a table or in a sandbox with or without words. Simple. Straightforward. Inviting. After a while, most at Redeemer participated in one way or another, at first in small groups and then in worship on Sunday mornings. Eventually, every council and congregational meeting ended with candle prayers. Somehow holding a candle, lighting it, and placing it with others became a powerful ritual connecting us with God and one another.

> Gradual steps in both prayer and organizing led to more shifts in the congregational life.

Gradual steps in both prayer and organizing led to more shifts in the congregational life. We moved from private stories to more public acknowledgment and participation in one another's stories. One way this happened was by organizing prayer circles.

Rhonda called one afternoon. "Pastor Moe, my husband and I have decided to move to Florida later this week. He hasn't found good work here, and his brother has offered him a job there. We have a motor home we can drive and have a cooler full of McDonald's hamburgers we bought on sale. We just don't have enough gas money to get there. Is there any way the church can help us out?"

"Sure. Of course. We have emergency funds. How much do you need?"

"$300 should be enough."

"OK, no problem. I'll get a check to you later this week. The treasurer is in tomorrow, and he can write the check." This had become a common practice at Redeemer, a private exchange between pastor and one in need. After I hung up, I was taken aback. Rhonda and A. J., her husband, were primary members of Redeemer. A. J. had been council president during a particularly difficult transition year, and both were on the core team we were developing. It didn't feel right to just give them the money and have them sneak out of town in the dead of night, leaving the congregation and relationships they had been a part of behind without a word. I called her back.

I told her we had the money and that I'd get it to them. But then I continued awkwardly, trying to find my words for a new thing: "Would you and A. J. be open to coming to Redeemer to meet with some of us to listen to your story and to pray with you? I could give you the check then." "Let me talk to my husband," she said. An hour later, the phone rang. "Yes," she said, "A. J. and I are open. What do you have in mind?" I looked at the calendar. It was Wednesday. They were leaving on Friday. "Could you come tomorrow at 4:00 p.m.? I'll call some of the members to be here then as well. Is that OK?"

I called a few people who knew A. J. and Rhonda, and they called a few others. When they walked into the chapel on that Thursday afternoon, fifteen people had assembled there. Before they came, I had instructed the circle not to pressure them to stay. "The purpose of our gathering is to listen to their story and to offer our support and love." I opened by reading a Psalm and saying a prayer. Then I asked Rhonda and A. J. to share what was in their hearts as we listened to their story. We heard how the pressures were mounting. We just listened. Then people shared their blessings, support, and love. Some tears began to show. After the meeting, I gave them a check for $300, and another member dug in his pocket and pulled out a hundred-dollar bill to give them. And we left. Strangely, I felt better. I was more comfortable with them leaving. It felt much less transactional between me and them. The congregation was in ministry, and a delicate problem had been opened up publicly.

The next morning, Rhonda called: "Pastor Moe, we decided not to move. We didn't realize we had such community here, and who knows what it would be like in Florida. Thank you." So began an entirely new community practice based both in our emerging organizing culture and our deepening spiritual life of prayer, meditation, and growing love. Over the years, many individuals and sometimes whole families would come to the chapel for prayer and reflection. Sometimes we called them "prayer circles," sometimes "reflection circles," sometimes "discernment circles." Often, I would initiate a circle with an invitation. Other times, someone would ask me or another leader to organize a circle for them. Sometimes a circle would be called spontaneously with the clinking of a cup at coffee hour.

We also began yearly retreats for leaders of Redeemer. These retreats became a source of strength and well-being as well as a sacred space for spiritual and relational growth. Redeemer was rich with both experienced and new leaders eager to reflect and grow together. Many, many prayer sessions lifted up the connections between the struggles of our members and our congregation as an institution while we began to recognize and name the mammoth public forces shifting beneath our feet. Full weekend retreats created space for transformation.

As these retreats evolved to include not just council leaders, but any who wanted to attend, they were planned and led by the core team, leaders active in organizing. This added a much needed relational, prayerful, and strategic dimension to the retreats. We discovered a sacred place on the Oregon coast: the Nestucca Sanctuary, a Jesuit-owned retreat center. It was rustic, with a large kitchen and dining area where we could cook our own food, and there were rooms for sleeping. A yurt, however, was its main attraction, located in the trees above the dining hall. We huddled around the fireplace in semidarkness for prayer, reflection, and relational/spiritual work in a tent of meeting, a sacred space where a sign invited us to take off our shoes as we entered holy ground.

These retreats grounded and inspired us for the work of transformation that was already happening, though at times seemed so elusive. The retreats also prepared us for the bumps and obstacles and even painful setbacks that often accompanied the journey to newness.

As we learned and implemented both organizing arts and practices and deepened corporate spiritual practices, Redeemer began to break open. Some of the hard nuts of congregational life—such as the isolation of individuals out of shame or fear of rejection or the dismissal of a political role for the church because "church and politics don't mix"—began to crack. Individuals did begin to share their stories, and a deeper community began to form. Candles, prayer circles, and retreats became ways to pay attention to a voice from the burning bush, to recognize the holy ground upon which we stood.

OUR FAMILY AND COMMUNITY

All this was going on in the congregation while the community continued to slide into increasing violence and blight. Multnomah County faced a thousand vacant and abandoned homes due to foreclosures or failure to pay taxes. Eight hundred of these houses were in the same zip code as Redeemer. What were once majestic Victorian homes were tattered and boarded up. Gangs and drug dealers took over whole neighborhoods. Threats of violence and uncertain housing markets created another wave of flight: this time both Blacks and whites who could afford to move often fled the neighborhood.

Our family stayed but continued to struggle with our adopted children. Both needed extended residential treatment, our daughter in Texas for nine months and our son in Oregon for six. It wracked our home with stress. Our daughter, who had first run away when she was twelve, never returned to live with us. Like a salmon swimming upstream, she lived in shelters, foster homes, on the street, and with my parents. She was pimped out when she was thirteen. Our social worker found her in the hospital with a jaw so badly broken, it had to be wired shut while it healed. My parents, who had taken her in after she left our home and her first treatment centers only to have her run away again, lured her to a bus terminal in Portland where my friend and I waited with the police to get her off the street. This was the second time we captured her like a frightened deer.

She spent nearly a year in a secure treatment center in San Marcos, Texas. We were required to visit every month or so. In one session, the psychiatrist in San Marcos, who like our daughter was a Native American, introduced our daughter to totem cards depicting the animal spirits. "I'm going to call it 'magic' for your daughter, but it is my way of getting to the root of some of her longings," she informed us. When she laid out her cards and turned over her primary totem, I thought for sure it would be a skunk or snake, we were so discouraged. Instead, it was a hummingbird. My wife and I both burst into tears when we discovered the soul of our tragically desperate daughter was a hummingbird. It fit so beautifully.

When our insurance ran out, she was pronounced stable and sent home. Within a month, she was on the street again. She went to Alaska to find her birth mother only to return a month later disappointed that she wasn't the dream mother she longed for. Finally, she returned to the reservation to live with relatives. Soon she was pregnant. She had just turned seventeen. We didn't know how to react to this news. It was the beginning of a long journey for her back to Native American life. For us it was yet another immersion in the Exodus story. As we came closer to the Native American world to which our daughter belonged, we better understood Hebrew people and the suffering they experienced at the hands of their Egyptian overseers.

HOLY GROUND FROM EAST TO WEST

I first heard of Pastor John Heinemeier in connection with the Nehemiah Housing project in Brooklyn, New York, via an article in the *Christian Century*. Ten years later, I saw his name again on a brochure from the ELCA inviting leaders to evangelism events in major cities across the country. St. John's Lutheran, the Bronx, where John then pastored, was the only inner-city congregation featured among all the other promising evangelism sites. I couldn't go to this event, but I hustled money, and Redeemer sent five leaders whom we dubbed the "Bronx Five." Three were younger Black leaders from Redeemer: Arvel Richardson, grandson of Vivian, and Trina and Marvin Barber, children of matriarch Laura Barber. The Bronx Five include two white leaders, 1993–94 intern Mary Amundson and Darrel King, who had been instrumental in the development of the Hallelujah Kids and constantly brought new people to Redeemer.

Investing in leaders such as these was now the prime objective of my ministry. The area of organizing "leadership development" opened to me. What I had been receiving from organizers and seasoned leaders I was now beginning to pay forward to interns, lay leaders, and other clergy.

A year later, I, too, would travel to the East Coast to meet our 1994–95 intern, Solveig Nilsen-Goodin, at Lutheran School of Theology Philadelphia. Since I was going so far, I tagged on a few extra days to make appointments with leaders from IAF organizations there, Philadelphia Interfaith Alliance and South Bronx Churches. I met with Rev. John Heinemeier of St. John's, where our delegation had been less than a year earlier, and with Rev. Heidi Neumark[9] of Transfiguration Lutheran, whom I had first seen in an inspiring ELCA video about her work in South Bronx, *Rattling Bones in the Bronx*. It just happened that South Bronx Churches was having an action assembly to negotiate with school officials on issues raised by parents. I was able to attend this assembly. Heidi and John became colleagues across the continent both in organizing and as intern supervisors.

I also worshipped at St. Paul Community Church in Brooklyn, where Rev. Johnny Ray Youngblood pastored a key IAF congregation

---

[9] Rev. Heidi Neumark is currently pastor of Trinity Lutheran, Manhattan. She is the author of two excellent books, both listed in the bibliography.

involved in Nehemiah housing and other important issues. Rev. Young-blood was cordial and invited me to meet with some of their leaders after a worship service. Pastor Ray autographed a copy of the book about his life and ministry, *Upon This Rock*,[10] and sent me off with a vision and blessing I'll never forget.

In prayer circles and testimonies in worship, in annual retreats, and in organizing workshops, Redeemer began to feel the significance of the bush all aflame, to turn toward it, and to hear the voice within the fire calling us to holy work.

FOR REFLECTION

The IAF ten-day leadership training impacted Pastor Moe greatly, really setting a new course for ministry.

- What experiences, books, retreats, workshops, ideas, and mentors have impacted you?
- How did these move you to discover and deepen your ongoing calling?

One-to-one relational meetings became the key new practice for Pastor Moe and eventually for the community.

- What key practices have evolved for you over time—specifically, in spirituality, organizational life, and social engagement?

[10] Samuel G. Freedman, *Upon This Rock: The Miracles of a Black Church* (New York: Harper Collins, 1993).

5 BECOMING MINDFUL OF THE PEOPLE

"I am," He said, "the God of your father, the God of Abraham, the God of Isaac, and the God of Jacob." And Moses hid his face, for he was afraid to look at God.[1]

—Exodus 3:6

Biblically speaking, the preeminent activity of the church is in the public arena, not in the sanctuary.[2]

—Dennis Jacobsen

Later on I discovered and am still discovering up to this day that one only learns to have faith by living in the full this-worldliness of life.[3]

—Dietrich Bonhoeffer

IN FEBRUARY 1994, POP WAS FORTUNATE TO HIRE DICK HARMON, AN experienced organizer from New York. Dick had been organizing thirty-five years, going back to the beginning of the modern IAF in 1961. He had worked closely with Saul Alinsky's successor, Ed Chambers, and helped develop the one-to-one meeting model. He was an excellent listener, organizer, and teacher. He really took to heart the value of organizing for the benefit of congregations and

---

[1] Exodus 3:6, JPS H-ET.

[2] Dennis Jacobsen, *Doing Justice: Congregations and Community Organizing*, 2nd ed. (Minneapolis: Fortress, 2017), 20.

[3] Dietrich Bonhoeffer, "Letter to Eberhard Bethge, July 21, 1944," in *Letters and Papers from Prison, Dietrich Bonhoeffer Works, English Edition*, vol. 8, ed. John W. de Gruchy, trans. Isabel Best, Lisa E. Dahill, Reinhard Krauss, and Nancy Lukens (Minneapolis: Fortress, 2010), 486.

other mediating institutions. Under his guidance, local twelve-hour leadership institutes began, in which local leaders were trained in and practiced many of the basic organizing concepts and skills taught at the IAF ten-day events. These institutes were scaled back for beginning leaders but were challenging nonetheless. The institutes provided key training and connections for each congregation to build core teams to build relationships and move to action. Later, groups engaged in more complex and engaging actions, which I will describe in this and subsequent chapters.

Over the years, Dick became a close mentor for me. He challenged me to increase my number of one-to-one meetings. He invited me into a discipline of writing weekly reflections to share with him and the organizing staff, Nancy Phelps from Redeemer and Chris Kresek, a lay leader from St. Rita Catholic. Chris had cochaired POP's founding assembly with me five years earlier. In writing these reflections, I thrived even as I was stretched.

FAMILY ERUPTIONS

On Father's Day in June 1994, a crazed gunman opened fire at a Fairchild Air Force Base hospital in Spokane, Washington, killing four people and injuring twenty-three, among them my first cousin, his wife, and two young daughters, ages fifteen and ten. The family has never recovered. I had grown up with this cousin, spending time together nearly every weekend and sharing meals every Thanksgiving, Christmas, and New Year's. We were close. He was in intensive care for thirty days with almost daily surgeries to repair his shattered hip and protect the sciatic nerve. My aunt Leona and uncle Lowell moved into an apartment nearby to accompany their son through the summer. I visited as often as I could, though Spokane was seven hours away. During one visit, my uncle took me by the hand and led me to his son's sedated body, "Terry, pray for my son," he pleaded. In the second offering of the leadership institutes, I was able to talk about this public/private tragedy.

At the end of that summer, more family tragedy struck. Our first granddaughter, Angelique, was stillborn, and her mother, our seventeen-year-old daughter, almost died as well. On a Wednesday in September 1994, I received a long-distance collect person-to-person phone call, something I'd come to expect from our daughter from time to time. "I'm in labor, and the baby's coming!" My mind whirled. Baby? Labor? Yes, I knew she was pregnant, but something wasn't adding up, because she was not due until December 5.

When we arrived, her water had broken, and she was fully dilated though only seven months along. The birthing crew was standing by. It was time to deliver. "Yes," the doctor told us, "it will be touch and go. Each hour is critical, but the labor is far along."

Our daughter had gone into premature labor because the baby inside her died. Now it was her life that was at risk. We stood beside her during the stillbirth. She had contracted E. coli and was running a 107-degree temperature. After the baby came out, they packed our daughter in ice and hooked her up to IVs to saturate her fevered body with fluids. Powerful antibiotics poured in to combat the infection racing through her bloodstream before it reached her critical organs: lungs, kidneys, liver, and heart. Death opened its door wide enough for us all to get a good look, but after three days in ICU fighting pneumonia and wrestling with her baby's death, she got better and began to make plans for the baby's funeral.

> As the river carried me through its gorge, I am taken back to my own journey: I am a desert-born, fir-forest-raised city dweller, a white male person of privilege, a parent and pastor in over my head, now living in complex diversity.

FALLING INTO THE INDIAN WORLD

Three times in ten days we drove the scenic Columbia Gorge to the Yakama Indian Reservation, where our daughter, a registered

Yakama tribal member, now lived. She went by her Indian name, Pansy Virginia James, though we still called her Tanja, the name we gave her when we adopted her as a three-month-old infant. Hers is a long story. Like the river, she's been over and through so much.

As the river carried me through its gorge, I am taken back to my own journey: I am a desert-born, fir-forest-raised city dweller, a white male person of privilege, a parent and pastor in over my head, now living in complex diversity. Who could have known the pain this cross-cultural adoption would inflict? How powerful the natural forces are! How paltry our parental love seemed at this time. We knew about Native American fishing rights when we adopted our daughter in 1977, but we knew nothing about fetal alcohol syndrome, which wasn't even named. We knew of prejudice and racism, but only from the outside, and we naively believed we could rise above it, as if our privilege included being lifted from a burning cauldron without being burned by the fire below. Our own personal pain would become public in the community of Redeemer, along with fiery brands from others' stories. I was, by our family's experience and in the multi-ethnic community of Redeemer, confronted by an angel who spoke from a fiery bush.

I didn't realize it then, but I was falling. I was falling into God and the world at the same time, this time through an Indian portal. The events of my life—the painful personal tragedies and the mercurial learning and development I embraced—sent my soul to depths I had never known and to heights I hadn't imagined. Redeemer began to shrink and get stronger. Finances were tough, and the community grew tougher. The seeds of transformation sank deep in the soil of my heart and in the heart of Redeemer, unseen yet powerfully present, to rise in other times. A rising spirituality embraced even this experience as our organizing acumen increased.

POWER

Dick Harmon was a strong teacher and organizer, challenging POP leaders and bringing a startling critique of the dominant culture that had lulled people into complacency while cities burned. Not everyone appreciated him. He became my primary mentor, and with his tutelage, I began to discover both the depths of story—my own and others'—and the powerful, often invisible forces of systems affecting many from behind closed curtains. While many of my colleagues delved into family systems theory to inform their ministries, I came to see that family systems were too small a frame to be really helpful. I read two Walters: Walter Brueggemann and Walter Wink. Both exposed in biblical and theological terms what I was discovering in organizing. Both impacted me through their books and also through their presentations at theological conferences I was able to attend. This statement by Frederick Douglass (1818–95) sums up the message succinctly: "Power concedes nothing without a demand. And it never will."[4]

Walter Brueggemann cracked open the Old Testament story in vivid terms of oppression, power, and domination on the one hand and amnesia, denial, and accommodation on the other. His themes of contrast between empire and people resound through his many books. Themes from his early classic, *The Prophetic Imagination*, reiterate and deepen in his later books. For example, in *Out of Babylon*, he clearly juxtaposes the story of empire and people's own struggles currently: "To appreciate fully that local tradition of prophetic poetry and liturgical response, we should contrast it with the empire's own liturgy. The empire's liturgy was all doxology, all praise, all celebration, all self-affirmation, and all victorious confidence. The empire had no room for sadness, loss, or grief. Unwelcome poetry never found voice in the empire, for the poets of unwelcome were all silenced. The empire permitted no cry, expected no response, engaged in no dialogue, offered no ultimate holiness . . . and so practiced an unrecognized despair and an uninterrupted denial."[5]

---

[4] This statement can be found in his "West India Emancipation" speech at Canandaigua, New York, on August 3, 1857. Douglass was born a slave. He escaped slavery to become active in the abolitionist movement and a suffragist. He is remembered as a statesman and a great orator.

[5] Walter Brueggemann, *Out of Babylon* (Nashville, TN: Abingdon, 2010), 53.

The fledgling Redeemer core team struggled to name, claim, and bring to the surface not only the groans and cries of our stories but their connectedness to societal structures. Walter Wink helped me ground these new experiences in Scripture and theology. His work named, unmasked, and engaged these often unconscious, unknown, invisible, unreflected upon, and therefore all the more powerful forces in his brilliant trilogy: *Naming the Powers* (1984), *Unmasking the Powers* (1986), and *Engaging the Powers* (1992).[6]

> The fledgling Redeemer core team struggled to name, claim, and bring to the surface not only the groans and cries of our stories but their connectedness to societal structures.

What was going on in the world in the 1990s as Redeemer leaders dove into the waters of story, interpretation, and connection? What were the invisible forces in Portland and nationally and internationally that affected our personal experiences? Why was it important to reflect on these public dimensions, so often relegated to the backwaters of our minds by currents of denial, confusion, and a sense of powerlessness?

Participants in the leadership institutes soon organized a strong core team. Many leaders rotated in and out of this team through the years, but they began not only to engage members around issues but to build relationships in the congregation across the many aisles that separated us. Those "aisles" separated elders and younger families, Black and white, rich and poor. The core team did the work of transformation inside the congregation even as we engaged bigger issues in the community.

Global tectonic plates shifted in the 1990s as well. In 1989, the Berlin Wall that since 1961 had divided that city with armed checkpoints and strict military enforcement began to crumble as relations between East and West Berlin thawed. By the end of 1991, the Soviet Union had dissolved into multiple democratic nations. In

[6] See the bibliography.

1992, El Salvador came to an uneasy truce in a decades-long civil war. After forty years of oppression for Black and mixed-race South Africans, apartheid ended in the early 1990s, and a new democratic government took shape in 1994 under President Nelson Mandela, who had been imprisoned for twenty-nine years. What did these global winds have to do with the rising spirituality and organizing that was blowing through Portland?

On the domestic front, Portland and other metropolitan areas were losing good manufacturing jobs, housing costs due to deregulation of banks began to surge, health care costs rose, people's income leveled off, and welfare reform put more stress on poor families. These were some of the shifts beginning to impact our families in Portland. At a regional IAF gathering, I learned this definition of organizing: "Organizing is the active unearthing of people's individual stories, the collective examination of the meaning of these stories in light of our shared story, and the opportunity to write new endings to both our individual and collective stories."[7]

Yes. Stories, unearthed, reflected upon in light of our tradition and shared stories, and moving us to action toward new histories yet to be written. We could be part of making all things new in Portland! That meant a new relationship with power. Power among can counterbalance the tendency of power over to corrupt. To avoid falling into that tendency ourselves, POP exercised shared leadership, appointing two or more leaders for every action and rotating leadership so as not to tap the same leaders all the time. Sharing and rotating leadership along with ongoing evaluation and reflection mitigated the tendency toward corruption in our own camp.

> Sharing and rotating leadership along with ongoing evaluation and reflection mitigated the tendency toward corruption in our own camp.

---

[7] Larry McNeil, West Coast regional director for IAF.

SHIFTS IN CONGREGATIONAL LIFE

In the spring of 1994, I flew to Los Angeles to meet with other IAF religious leaders around how organizing might impact congregations. Larry McNeil, the West Coast director for IAF, led the sessions. His first question was "What kind of congregation would give you life?" Together we brainstormed a list of responses that he outlined on the board in front of us. Then he challenged us by asking, "What kind of leadership could bring about the kind of congregations we would like to see?"

Together we created matrices of organizational shift and of pastoral modes of operation to make shifts happen (see appendix 2). I put these matrices in plain view above my desk as I immediately recognized that if I wanted the congregation to shift and be transformed, I had to operate in a different manner. I carried this shift in my mind and heart through many years of organizing in Redeemer. What I was learning in actions in the community reflected back on our own unearthing of our stories, including our congregational story, and how we might write new endings. How was I developing as a leader/organizer while also performing the duties of a traditional pastor? How were others being developed as leaders? What did we need to let go in order to shift? How could we do different things and do things differently?

UNVEILING POWER IN PORTLAND

Dick would lead us to uncover one of Portland's hidden power dimensions as we engaged the Central City 2000 Task Force (CCTF). CCTF was established in the fall of 1994. Its charge was to promote a strong and vibrant downtown, something no one could really oppose, though we soon discovered this meant more for those who already have and less for the rest. The Central City 2000 Task Force became our teacher and led us to deep engagement with the powers of Portland. We were apprentices learning to act for the interests and values of our congregations on a big screen. This was mostly outside our experience; hidden, at first; and even daunting, as we as leaders of POP waded in over our heads.

The *Oregonian*, Portland's weekly and Oregon's main newspaper, did POP a huge favor: it published the names, positions, and pictures of the CCTF on the front page of its business section in the spring of 1994.[8] Dick immediately recognized the gift that had been handed to us, though many of us had no inkling of what it meant. Here was a who's who of Portland power brokers: CEOs, business and government bigwigs, presidents, and "kings." These were people of power experienced in running big organizations and used to getting their way.

In the leadership institutes, hundreds of leaders eagerly learned the dynamics of public life. Dick shed light on some of the intricacies of those behind the term "smoke-filled rooms" and the adage "You can't fight city hall." POP had already successfully negotiated shifts in sewer, police, and derelict housing policies at the government level and had dipped our toes into the arena of corporate power through the Fred Meyer negotiation. Now the two formidable forces of government and market coalesced in the Central City 2000 Task Force. What was missing in most of the planning efforts in most major cities, including Portland? Who was not at the table as major decisions affecting the whole landscape of the city were forged? Ordinary people! That's what POP brought to public life. Ordinary people like me, now awakened and aware, ready for action.

> That's what POP brought to public life. Ordinary people like me, now awakened and aware, ready for action.

Dick organized leaders to attend Central City 2000 Task Force meetings being held in a conference room of Northwest Natural Gas. Mr. Robert Ridgely was the CEO and chair of the CCTF. In groups of fifty or sixty, POP leaders sat in the audience month after month,

---

[8] See appendix 3 for a listing of members of CCTF.

listening, observing, and reflecting as the CCTF conducted its business in a U-shape configuration with microphones and the latest Power-Point and recording technologies. Then after an hour or so, we would leave and convene in the lobby for a standing evaluation. "What did you notice?" Mr. Harmon asked. "Who are the leaders running the show? What are their interests and plans? What is the role of the mayor in this setting?" and so forth. We began to witness the layers of corporate strategy most often conducted in the high and inaccessible offices or behind the closed doors of the Multnomah Athletic Club.[9] Clearly, Mr. Ridgely was the power in the room as he chaired the meeting, while the mayor, Vera Katz, mostly sat quietly next to him.

The Central City 2000 Task Force operated for eighteen months, carefully looking at a vision of a renewed downtown featuring a new light rail, trolleys, renovations of existing buildings, and most importantly two new urban renewal districts (URDs): the River District, which would become the "Pearl" in Northwest Portland, and South Waterfront, which was soon to follow in Southwest Portland. Designated URDs benefited from tax-increment funding (TIF).[10] I was learning the lessons of public life along with many leaders from Redeemer and other congregations. We didn't have a Multnomah Athletic Club, but we had POP.

It would have been easy for me and others to fall into demonizing corporations because I knew little about them and had formed opinions based on prejudice and the lack of a firsthand relationship. Dick Harmon would have nothing to do with demonizing, critical as he was. Paraphrasing the attitude of Walter Wink, Dick suggested,

[9] For more on MAC, see https://themac.com/web/pages/about-mac.

[10] TIF was a key component of urban renewal districts (URD), providing necessary funding for new development. The current property tax in a designated URD was frozen at the rate when the URD was established. For the next twenty years, the amount of tax assessed that resulted from increased value of the property, the increment, went not to general taxes for schools, police, and fire, as it normally would, but to an urban renewal fund to be used exclusively for development within the URD boundaries. While this had historically benefited blighted urban areas in cities across the country, its current use tended to benefit developers and financial institutions, especially when the land being designated was vacant and therefore subject to exponential increases in its value as it was developed, and hence a lot of money was directed to the URD's funds.

"Corporate executives aren't evil; they're just out of touch with the people, confused by their power." I reflected on how the powerful tend toward corruption when unrestrained by community and how the powerless tend also to be corrupted when they cease to be engaged with power. Both power and powerlessness tend toward corruption in a malevolent cycle, a system of degeneration and injustice. A core understanding of power and its corollary powerlessness is taught regularly in local, regional, and national IAF leadership trainings. Ernesto Cortes Jr., director for IAF West/Southwest, makes the point clearly: "Ernesto Cortes, Jr., a highly regarded community organizer from San Antonio, Texas, has observed that Lord Acton's oft-quoted aphorism—'power tends to corrupt . . .'—works both ways. 'Power-lessness also corrupts,' Cortes said. 'We've got a lot of people who've never developed an understanding of power. They've been institution-ally trained to be passive. Power is nothing more than the ability to act on your own behalf. In Spanish, we call the word *poder*, to have capacity, to be able.'"[11]

IAF's response to this degrading cycle is to build nonpartisan power, to balance the equation, to act collectively on family values and interests in the large arena of politics through negotiation and the art of compromise. This requires education in democracy, teach-ing the skills of politics with a small *p*, and training in the disciplines of public life where values and interests are negotiated usually with-out strong input from the civil sector. This includes how to address public officials as decision makers, formally and respectfully, but also firmly and with confidence.

After the third or fourth meeting, POP planned a move, asking for time on the agenda of the next meeting. Father Jack Mosbrucker approached the microphone to lay out the vision POP had been working on, the Family Investment Trust, an alternative vision that invested in ordinary families for affordable housing and living-wage jobs throughout the city. He then asked for a meeting of POP leaders

[11] William Greider, *Who Will Tell the People? The Betrayal of American Democracy* (New York: Simon and Schuster, 1992), 20.

with Mr. Ridgely. POP's stance was that we would not oppose the development plans for downtown if corporate and city officials would work with POP to increase affordable housing and family-wage jobs throughout the city. Dick called it a "grand bargain."

I wasn't sure what the next step should be after observing and reflecting on the public meetings of the Central City 2000 Task Force and interjecting POP's vision and goals. "Time for one-to-ones with the key leaders at the CCTF table," Dick announced. Of course! I guess I should have known, but I couldn't imagine meeting with a major CEO of anything. It was so outside of my experience and imagination. Having announced POP goals publicly, leaders of POP went to work. Over the next several months, POP leaders met with corporate and government leaders individually from around the table to clarify our interests and to establish rapport. We met in teams of two or three in order to maximize the learning of our leadership as well as to demonstrate the depth and diversity of our organization. While we were learning not to demonize these high-powered leaders, we were also learning that they lacked experience in dealing with organized citizens too. It was an awkward dance at first. We also sent delegations to some of the subcommittees of CCTF, including the River District Steering Committee, which was overseeing the development of one of the new urban renewal districts in the plan that would become the Pearl as well as convening meetings of the six industrial districts in Portland where the economic opportunities of the master plan were applied and expanded.

Dick laid out a schedule of individual meetings with the leaders at the CCTF table. He calmly organized teams to call on the key decision makers: Robert Ridgely, the chair of the CCTF and CEO of Northwest Natural Gas as well as the president of the Oregon Business Council, the most prestigious and powerful big business alliance in Oregon. We met with Fred Buckman, CEO of PacifiCorp, a regional utility covering seven states with annual gross revenue of $3.4 billion in 1994, and bank presidents who had interests in the urban renewal developments. I was assigned to the team to meet with Mr. Buckman. Others met with Mr. Ridgely or other leaders from around the table. We were exercising an important capacity for organizing: organized people.

Why would they meet with us? Because fifty citizens walked into a public set of meetings required to be open by law to observe and learn. Because many of the corporate leaders were interested in the common good. That included Bob Ridgely, a powerful "city father" and well respected by his peers. He had brokered big real estate deals including Pioneer Court House Square downtown and the new Trail Blazers stadium in Northeast Portland. He was also a local leader who was invested in the community. He had gone to Central Catholic High School and had raised his family in Portland. When our POP team met with him, one of the team, a sister of the Holy Names who had taught at Central Catholic, greeted him, "Hi, Bobby!" Others cooperated with POP because they knew the CCTF business was a public process and didn't want disruption to their plans.

Dick patiently taught us how to arrange the meeting: you call them up and make an appointment. In private sessions, he tutored us on what we would encounter. "This is Rev. Moe from Portland Organizing Project. Can I speak to the person who schedules meetings for Mr. Buckman?" Each step was an amazing unfolding of a reality I knew existed but hadn't experienced. The sixteenth-floor office of the CEO of PacifiCorp is a far cry from my small study at Redeemer. I learned that CEOs have personal lives, as one meeting had to be postponed because of a burst pipe at his home in the West Hills due to an ice storm. I learned that he had played tight end for the Michigan Wolverines and that he was a nuclear physicist by training. While our worlds were far apart in some ways, we were also connected in other ways. As we sat in his office, I was dressed in my best suit and tie, and he in a sharp, no doubt expensive, tieless blue shirt and dress slacks. But we met and developed a public relationship.

Sometimes it wasn't that easy. Sometimes POP leaders had to take actions to get the attention of decision makers, who like the bankers early on would as soon put their feet up on the table as take ordinary people seriously. Saul Alinsky taught that the purpose of action was to get a reaction, most often an exchange of power in a relationship of mutual respect. Sometimes this meant confrontation. To confront means to "put our foreheads together" in close proximity but not in violence. We were learning that organizing was an alternative to violence that sometimes erupts out of frustration and a sense of powerlessness, on one hand, or a cavalier sense of power, on the other, accountable to no one. That can be violence as well. In addition to our meetings with CCTF leaders, others met with various committees of the process. One such committee was the River District Steering Committee.

Businessmen, developers, landowners in the district, investors, and real estate brokers all had special—and many had vested—self-interest in the developments of the urban renewal districts all along the Willamette River. For example, many members of the steering committee owned property in the area, had invested in the development process, or stood to benefit from it in tangible ways. The River District Steering Committee oversaw the urban renewal district on the north side of downtown that would soon become the Pearl. The committee was stacked with bankers and developers who had a stake in its success. They had money on the table, as they had already invested hundreds of thousands in the developments. Clearly the steering committee had the interests of these in mind. POP wanted to insert the interests of working-class folks and people who lived outside what was to become an elite enclave. In ten short years, what was vacant industrial land would develop into a chic and thriving new community for over five thousand households, sporting fashionable microbrew bars, wine shops, restaurants, and boutiques and connected by trolley, streetcar, and light rail to downtown and the airport as well as suburbs to the west. This vision was held by the River District Steering Committee and the promise of urban renewal money, adding to other public and private investment and bringing the total to over a billion dollars in all the downtown projects. While the city can be lauded for looking ahead and not letting Portland follow the course of Detroit, Pittsburgh, or other major cities devastated by economic shifts and neglect, POP leaders had other interests and values to bring to the table.

Along the way, POP leaders had been informed that all the public money available for affordable housing in Portland was being sucked into the River District and its sister, South Waterfront, leaving the rest of the city without resources to meet the ever-increasing housing affordability crisis now raising its head. We had been hearing stories about the need for affordable housing in our congregations, and now this information was confirmed by statistical data from the city and state. Incomes were flat. Housing prices were rising. Our people were caught in a vise. Something had to be done. So leaders staged an action, a public intervention on business as usual, at the River District Steering Committee.

POP leaders, clergy in clerical collars and laypeople dressed for a public event, arrived early for the meeting and took seats around the big table in the center of the conference room where the committee held its monthly "public" meetings. When members of the committee arrived late because of traffic after their lunch together, they at first were confused. "Who are these people sitting in our chairs?" Then they were angry. "What are you doing here? This is our meeting!" One red-faced developer stood up and started to berate us in a loud voice with intimidating gestures. I was paralyzed, but nobody moved, so I didn't either. Then out of the corner of my eye, I saw Rev. James Smith, pastor of Allen Temple Christian Methodist Episcopal Church, stand up and assume a position directly across the table from where the chair was still spouting in frustration. Without raising his voice but in measured cadence, he explained, "We are leaders from Portland Organizing Project. We are citizens of Portland who work and pay taxes. We understand that considerable public money is going into this project, and we have a stake in how that money is spent. We have an interest in what's going on here because we understand that all of the public money for affordable housing is going to this side of the river, and we don't like it. We need affordable housing on the other side of the river where our people live. We're here to see what we can do about it."

Later in the negotiating process, POP had a meeting with Portland development staff and Sam Adams, the chief of staff of the City of Portland, the second most powerful city figure, who eventually was elected mayor. We met in the mayor's meeting room behind closed doors. I sat at the head of the table, with Dick to my left and Portland Development Commission staffer Lisa Neisenfeld across the table from Dick. When Mr. Adams came in, he immediately noticed where I was sitting and said, "That's the mayor's place. It's where I sit when she's not here." He steamed a little. I didn't move. He excused himself, saying that he had to get his folder from his office, likely offering me the chance to move to the other side of the table. When he came back, I hadn't budged. "Well, this meeting is getting off to a great start," he fumed as he took a place at the table. It wasn't the most important thing in the world, but for some reason, I got my dander up. I was experimenting in holding a seat of power, disrupting the routine, standing up for myself and our people—all things Rev. Smith had modeled for me.

I learned from Rev. Smith, and later I would assume positions at other tables of power, sometimes unwelcomed. I thought how Rev. Smith's posture and stature, like that of Martin Luther King Jr., had grown out of the suffering of slavery, Jim Crow, and modern racism. On the rising tide of a solid spirituality sung in Gospel music, prayed through in revivals and propagated by powerful preaching, he and others were forged for dealing with power. I was learning how organizing grew out of oppression, going back to the days of slavery in Africa, back to Moses, who first heard God say, "Let my people go."

SPIRITUALITY AND THE SUFFERING OF GOD

Somehow, mysteriously and fortuitously, another brochure came to my attention in the spring of 1995: "Spirituality and the Suffering of God." It was a doctor of ministry program, offered jointly by Wesley Theological Seminary, Washington, DC, and the Upper Room, Nashville, Tennessee. I read the brochure that included a short description and layout of the program:

- six two-week sessions, some at Wesley and some at the Upper Room
- one two-week immersion experience in one of three options: Holocaust sites, South Africa, or El Salvador
- reading, writing, and reflection, including a one-hundred-page project thesis

I wasn't interested in another degree, but like "Introduction to Spiritual Living" in 1983, I felt called to participate. I wasn't interested in a program, but it offered me a chance to reflect and write on my nearly ten years of experience in spirituality and organizing. Here was a seminary course that took seriously the connection between academics and spirituality. Here was a program that seemed grounded in hard realities and the struggle for liberation as expressed in immersion experiences. I was in! The seminary had received over eighty applications for forty slots, far exceeding their expectations. I was accepted.

In August 1995, I flew to Washington, DC, for the first session, where I met with thirty-five colleagues from all over the US, most of whom were seasoned pastors and theologians from all denominations. The following winter, I traveled to Nashville, where I met and began to appreciate my advisor, Rueben Job, spiritual sage and leader of the Upper Room. My first teacher was Marjorie Thompson, author of a recently published book, *Soul Feast: An Invitation to the Christian Spiritual Life.*[12] In the spring of 1996, I was off to El Salvador for my chosen immersion experience. I ate it up. I was learning so much on the ground in POP and at Redeemer, and having time to integrate and reflect through this program was a godsend. I graduated in May 1998 and presented my thesis, "O Healing River: Just Prayer and Organizing."

---

[12] Marjorie Thompson, *Soul Feast: An Invitation to the Christian Spiritual Life* (Louisville, KY: Westminster / John Knox, 1995).

Our portion of the doctor of ministry cohort, about fifteen of us, traveled to El Salvador in May 1996. It was even more devastating than what I witnessed in South Central Los Angeles after the Rodney King riots in 1992. We witnessed the twisted remains of civil war in El Salvador as communities struggled to recover. We were not there for sightseeing; with our seasoned guide, Professor Hal Recinos, who had led expeditions to El Salvador ten times before, we met local priests, organizers, and leaders of all kinds of development efforts. One leader was creating solar cookers so that folks could cook their beans in large pots by the power of the sun alone. Another developed a home for houseless children orphaned by the war. Another built a school. Another created a people's university to teach self-reliance and build community.

The backbone and strength of El Salvador, however, was in the church and the base communities initiated by priests and lay delegates of the word throughout Latin America with or without the blessing of the church's hierarchy. Since the assassination in 1980 of Archbishop Oscar Romero, who was gunned down by military snipers while celebrating Mass in a small hospital church, the people organized in his memory. In November 1989, six Jesuit priests teaching at the University of San Salvador were dragged out of bed at five a.m., marshaled to the grounds outside their modest dorms, and shot in the head. This act of horrendous violence was intended to kill the spiritual and organizing message they preached along with their bodies. We paid homage to Archbishop Romero in a basement church and at the hospital apartment where he had lived, eschewing the extravagant archbishop's mansion. We stood silently in the rose garden where the six Jesuit priests were assassinated not even a decade earlier. Such oppression. Such violence. Still the people rose. Still the people rise.

> "After returning from El Salvador in May of 1996 a simple summary of spirituality occurred to me: 'following Jesus and walking with the people.'"

I wrote in my thesis, "After returning from El Salvador in May of 1996 a simple summary of spirituality occurred to me: 'following Jesus and walking with the people.' Following Jesus is not disconnected from Scripture and prayer, but neither is it separate from walking with the people. To follow Jesus and to walk with the people implies a social spirituality, a conversion not just of individual souls, but of the society."[13]

Following Jesus and walking with the people became a mantra for the organizing and spirituality rumbling in my soul. Gustavo Gutierrez, the father of Latin American liberation theology whom I had read in seminary, writes,

> The change called for is not simply an interior one but one that involves the entire person as a corporeal being (a factor of human solidarity, as we saw when considering Pauline texts, above) and therefore also has consequences for the web of social relationships of which the individual is a part. That is why Archbishop Romero could make this strong statement: "Nowadays an authentic Christian conversion must lead to an unmasking of the social mechanisms that turn the worker and the peasant into marginalized persons. Why do the rural poor become part of society only in the coffee- and cotton-picking seasons? The will to conversion should lead to this kind of concrete analysis."[14]

I found myself weaving in and out of Redeemer, POP, and my doctor of ministry work, all of which I devoured with a burning passion. The fire burned, and I was not consumed.

---

[13] Moe, "O Healing River," 66–67.
[14] Gustavo Gutierrez, *We Drink from Our Own Wells: The Spiritual Journey of a People* (Maryknoll, NY: Orbis, 1984), 98.

FOR REFLECTION

Power is an important concept biblically, theologically, in organizational culture, and in the world as it is and ought to be.

- What is your gut reaction to the concept of power?
- How have your thinking and actions shifted, if they have?
- How can a leader or leaders best bring life to a congregation?
- Reflect on the leadership shift chart in appendix 2. Where are you now? What kind of leader are you?
- Where would you like to be?
- How might you make shifts to get there?
- What things might you need to let go of, add, or blend in over time?

6 BRICKS, STRAW, AND A RED PIANO

And the Lord continued, "I have marked well the plight of My people in Egypt and have heeded their outcry because of their taskmasters; yes, I am mindful of their sufferings."[1]

—Exodus 3:7

Difficult as the pulpit job is, it is easier than the work in the organizations of the congregation.[2]

—Reinhold Niebuhr

Grief and repentance are the proper antidotes for the culture of denial and cover-up that has so permeated our church and wider society.[3]

—Kester Brewin

TREMENDOUS POWER SHIFTS THAT JOLTED PORTLAND AND THE WORLD began to appear in the 1990s. POP had local successes and was learning the ins and outs of political life in a midsize West Coast city. POP had successes at the turn of the millennium. It mitigated the costs of a huge public works project and provided for a safety net for low-income folks who were forced to join Portland's combined sewer overflow system. Additionally, it confronted two gigantic urban renewal projects to bring both fairer labor practices

---

[1] Exodus 3:7, JPS H-ET.
[2] Niebuhr, *Leaves from the Notebook*, 10.
[3] Kester Brewin, *Signs of Emergence: A Vision for Church That Is Organic/Networked/Decentralized/Bottom-Up/Communal/Flexible (Always Evolving)* (Grand Rapids, MI: Baker, 2007), 53.

and more affordable housing to these marquee new developments. At the same time, however, gigantic shifts deregulated banks and utilities politically while corporations gained power by nationalizing and globalizing. The effect of both of these was to present a much more formidable and elusive opponent at the negotiating table for the common good. These pressures affected individuals for sure, but more importantly, increasing pressure mounted on congregations, public schools, and labor unions alike. It was like people were being asked to gather their own straw and make more bricks just to get by.

THE PUBLIC DIMENSION OF OUR STORIES

While growing in openness to sharing our burdens in small groups and in Sunday liturgy, Redeemer began to lift up and reflect upon the public dimensions of our personal stories. How were our struggles not only of our own making but the result of political and economic realities? How did a new and more distant level of power affect us in ways we couldn't easily recognize or act upon? What could be done about it? And more importantly, we began to see cracks in our own congregation that could not be plastered over. We began to ask questions about our own power and powerlessness in the midst of a sea of change all around us.

In the late 1990s, Portland and the country as a whole experienced a corporate power shift. In a process known as deregulation, corporations used their lobbying power to pass national legislation designed to loosen financial regulations imposed after the Great Depression or during the New Deal and to undo ecological restrictions protecting the environment since Earth Day, 1970. For example, the Glass-Steagall Act, enacted by the US Congress as part of the 1933 Banking Act, was mostly repealed in the 1999 Gramm-Leach-Bliley Act. Deregulation and globalization continued through the decades in a process called financialization, allowing banks, financial investment firms, and insurance companies to merge, broaden, and invent new ways to make money in the stock market regardless of traditional banking roles in the community. The 3 percent return on passbook savings and the 4 percent local home loan became a thing of the past as mortgages were sold and resold, bundled into derivatives, and peddled on Wall Street, causing hyperinflation. The bubble burst in 2007–8, and the government bailed out corporations too big to fail, while homeowners lost their homes. Deregulation of utilities allowed massive power moves by utilities eager to consolidate and control growing energy markets while often sidestepping or ignoring environmental impacts. The prime example of this in Portland was the 1997 takeover of Portland General Electric (PGE) by Enron, a Texas-based energy firm, which ended in a well-publicized disaster.

POP had worked hard to establish working relationships with major corporations during the Family Investment Trust campaign. In May of 1998, at the largest assembly ever organized by POP, over nine hundred members of POP congregations gathered outdoors on the west bank of the Willamette River, site of the new urban renewal district, to celebrate a handshake deal with city and corporate leaders. POP agreed not to oppose the URDs; city and corporate leaders agreed to a plan to fund affordable housing across the city, totaling fifteen million a year for ten years. It was a grand bargain.

Then in the twinkling of an eye, the deal unraveled. Ownership of every major utility and bank in Portland shifted to national or international corporations, sometimes shifting multiple times, making it difficult to gain access to decision makers. After just two years of funding, the deal was moot. The whole CCTF table dissolved. Many retired. Others were displaced by the shift from local to national ownership. This growing trend had ramifications for members of Redeemer, our Redeemer congregation, other congregations, and POP.

Members of Redeemer were directly affected by corporate decisions whether they knew it or not. Leo, a retired career army veteran, went to work for a union company that made wooden pipes. The company was bought out, the union was busted, and workers were invited back at half the wages and minimal benefits. He stayed a while and then retired. Scott was not so fortunate. He worked for a unionized lumber mill as a sawyer, a skilled position with good wages and benefits. When his mill was bought out and the union decertified, he went to work at a hardware store, and his wife had to go back to work to make ends meet. Arnold worked as a union electrician for Portland General Electric for his whole career. He was happily retired. When Enron bought PGE, it required all retirement investments to be shifted into Enron stocks. Arnold and his wife, Margaret, lost his whole retirement in the Enron fiasco a few years later.

In reflection, the core team kept asking, "What are the public dimensions of these stories? Why is this happening? And what can we do about it?" Answering these questions was hard work for us who had been taught not to blame others for our problems. Public pressures on families were increasing across the country, something those in other countries readily understood, but for us, it was new. How could we open up the stories of those affected by market decisions in order to fight back?

These were but some of the stories the core team heard when engaging the congregation with the question "What pressures are you and your loved ones currently facing?" Of course, people were reluctant to share personal stories, especially those that seemed like failures. We were crossing the line of church and politics. We were asking people for a new level of engagement with each other. We were inviting a new kind of vulnerability into the sanctuary, a place many had fled into to avoid just such pressures. Organizing taught us a way to engage the suffering of these people from the ground up.

First, in one-to-ones, some stories were shared. Next, in small groups, people began to realize that they were not alone in experiencing these pressures. Eventually some stories became more public in testimonies during worship or at POP assemblies. Naming the public pressures connected to people's private struggles became the central task of the core leaders of Redeemer and other POP congregations. It was difficult work to unearth these painful stories and even more daunting to find ways to write new endings to what people were experiencing. In many congregations, people are equipped to deal with their situations as best they can with their own resources. This takes spiritual power as well as social skill and wisdom. To invite people into collective reflection and action, however, is almost unheard of in most congregations. It asks for a more public spirituality, a spirituality foreign to many. Redeemer was stepping over the line.

The seismic forces of globalization and the early signs of financialization rocked Portland. In order to confront larger statewide and national forces, leaders of POP voted to reorganize in 1998, shifting from an eastside, congregation-based organization to a tricounty, broad-based organization, including suburban and rural counties surrounding the Portland metro. The new organization also invited labor unions, school affiliates, community-based nonprofits, and diverse religious groups to join. The late 1990s exerted tremendous pressure on households, including rising housing, energy, and education costs, while at the same time, there was downward pressure on wages and less job security.

Just as individuals felt these pressures, so did Redeemer and all the congregations in POP. These pressures were global. IAF Northwest initiated new organizing affiliates in Spokane; Vancouver, British Columbia, Canada; and Seattle/Tacoma in the early 2000s, even as POP reformed as Metropolitan Alliance for Common Good (MACG) in 2002. We were beginning to understand how the changing world around us affected everything, including the congregation's identity and mission. We began to think about how the culture of the congregation needed to shift to confront new realities globally and locally. It has been said that it took only weeks for the Israelites to get out of Egypt,

> We were beginning to understand how the changing world around us affected everything, including the congregation's identity and mission.

but it took forty years to get Egypt out of the Israelites. For us at Redeemer, building power to confront the issues in the neighborhood began to curve back upon us.

We began to wonder how the arts and practices, mindset, network of relationships, and culture of relational power could be turned toward congregational renewal. How might stronger liturgy, deeper prayer, and spiritual exercises impact the DNA of a working-class, mostly white congregation in a changed and changing neighborhood?

Redeemer was not growing numerically. Yet we felt vital. Each year was a struggle to make ends meet and to stay fresh. Yet we were maturing in deeper spirituality and growing together in our practices of organizing. Many of the congregations in our neighborhood that had once been strong began a steady and precipitous slide into oblivion. Some closed. Some merged. Some continued to limp along. For a full decade, Redeemer also tottered on the brink of decline. What made the difference for Redeemer? Why did Redeemer survive in order to reinvent itself? When asked, our leaders replied, "Because of organizing, we had relationships, and we had hope." That is a spiritual and organizing answer. The two dimensions of the burning bush were coming together.

In 1997, Redeemer planted a time capsule in the form of a document compiled by council president Joan Lepley. It was called "What Were We Thinking in 1997?" It is a curious snapshot of Redeemer in the throes of transition, confusion, bewilderment, and hope. A sampling follows: "Redeemer is struggling to reinvent itself. We are all hoping and praying the church will find a new direction and renewed energy from its members."[4]

While Redeemer's core leadership team had been instrumental in moving the congregation out into action with other congregations in the neighborhood, now it was challenged to turn organizing inward to address our own transformation. Our growing understanding and implication of organizing invited regular one-to-ones by me and key core team leaders, house meetings, reading/reflection groups, and an evaluation of the congregation. These actions began to shift the culture of our congregation. At the beginning of 1998, I committed to making ten relational meetings a week for the forty days of Lent.

---

[4] Internal Redeemer document: "What Were We Thinking in 1997?"

After Lent, I found this practice so rewarding and life giving that I continued the practice until my retirement, fifteen years later. It was the single most impactful decision I made as a pastor/leader.

Redeemer's core team listened, discerned, acted, and reflected in, with, and under the congregation for almost a decade. Toward the end of the period, two episodes pulled back the curtain on Redeemer's vulnerability. First, a frustrating vote on a grand piano, a seemingly mundane setback, really showed a community divided. Second, and I'll get to that in the next chapter, a planned retreat featuring a simulated funeral for the church put the core team and congregation to the test and challenged us to live up to our belief in the resurrection.

The Worship and Music Committee performed due diligence and found a beautiful six-foot ebony grand piano at the local Moe's Pianos (no relation, but you have to love the coincidence!). They agreed to deliver and set it up for six weeks free of charge, after which we could make a decision. The asking price was $10,000. Prepledges from the council and committee leaders secured over $6,000 toward the cost. Leaders were optimistic that after six weeks of hearing the sweet timbre of the piano and having 60 percent of the cost covered, the vote would be a shoo-in.

At the congregational meeting, the motion was made and seconded. Then things unraveled.

"Do we really need a big, beautiful piano?"
"We are a small urban church. It seems extravagant."
"Shouldn't we put the money into feeding the hungry?"

And so forth . . .

Finally, the vote was taken. 19–19. It failed on a tie. The leadership was bewildered. Some were in tears. What in the world was going on?

Then the core team began to reflect on what had happened. "What does this mean?" they wondered. "We've got a chasm in the church," someone said.

"Yes. Nineteen on one side, and nineteen on the other," added another.

"Yes, but there are nineteen others in the middle who didn't come to the meeting or couldn't decide how they felt," said another.

"Sure. And there are nineteen ghosts of the past members pulling us backward."

"And nineteen potentially new members who might like a nice piano even in a poor church!"

A preliminary power analysis began to emerge: 19–19–19–19–19. Someone went to the easel and drew a chasm with the number *19* on one side and *19* on the other, adding the *19* in the middle and off to the sides:

TABLE 6.1. The redeemer chasm

	19 for	
19 ghosts of the past	19 in the middle	19 future saints
	19 against	

Then the core team began to face reality: "We have a chasm in our church!" They began to consider what to do. Looking back, I see this situation as a classic sign of what Heifetz identifies as an adaptive challenge. In identifying an adaptive challenge, he points to a "persistent gap between aspirations and reality."[5] The chasm in the church is not an unfamiliar reality, but it is often a hidden one. Now the red piano vote ripped the curtain open, revealing a gap between who we were and who we wanted to become. The core team immediately applied organizing principles to address the gap.

"We need to set up one-to-ones with the nineteen *against* and the nineteen *for* and all the other nineteens!" And they did. They organized one-to-ones to begin to understand more deeply the points

[5] Ron Heifetz, Alexander Grashow, and Marty Linksy, *The Practice of Adaptive Leadership: Tools and Tactics for Changing Your Organization and the World* (Boston: Harvard Business Press, 2009), 74.

of view in Redeemer, not to persuade people, but to build relationships, to begin discerning how people were feeling and what values they really held.

A couple of weeks after the piano vote, I was in Roslyn's Garden Coffee Shop on Alberta Street telling the proprietor, whom I had gotten to know, the story of the grand piano and the congregational vote. Then for some reason (frustration, desperation, wishful thinking, prayer?), I concluded by asking, "You don't know anyone who has a piano for sale, do you?" She smiled. A minute later, she emerged with a three-by-five photo. It was a bright-red baby grand piano! I thought, *The congregation deserves this!* She was willing to sell it for $3,200. We set up a six-week trial period similar to the initial grand piano from Moe's. When we brought the proposal to the congregation, it was approved unanimously.

That's how Redeemer got a red piano that still serves Leaven / Salt and Light. According to Roslyn, who bought the piano in Oakland, there is a twin red baby grand piano that belonged to and toured with Diana Ross of the Supremes. Redeemer and the Supremes! How 'bout that? More importantly, that's how the leadership of the core team and council began to deepen relationships in preparation for more important decisions to come. In fact, a decade later, in 2009, when Redeemer was getting serious about launching a new mission that would become Leaven / Salt and Light, the congregation had seven official congregational meetings on a variety of issues, including allocating proceeds from property sales (potentially $500,000, or fifty times the cost of the ebony grand piano). The votes were near unanimous every time, 29–3, 32–3, 34–1, and so forth. That's how a red piano changed a church!

The red piano crisis offered Redeemer an opportunity. We were learning that the congregation as a whole needed to be brought along. Early on, I had become aware that while the council was an important component for maintaining a congregation, it was not always the best vehicle to lead change. The piano story revealed a chasm between leaders and the rest of the congregation that manifested in a tie vote. More importantly, it revealed a community that was not on the same page, that didn't have deep, trusting relationships with each other and was not prepared to do anything about it.

At the same time, we were exploring a concept from Walter Brueggemann—the public processing of grief, a concept he connects directly to the exodus story. Brueggemann contends that our individual and corporate grief needs to be publicly processed for healing and liberation to occur. Organizing helped us do this, but it certainly challenged the many of us who were steeped in individual spirituality.

> By "public processing" I refer to an intentional and communal act of expressing grievance which is unheard of and risky under any absolutist regime. The faith-forming story has its second phase, "and we cried out." Think what a subversive, revolutionary move that is! It is not revolutionary to experience pain. The regime does not deny the reality of pain. Or, if one notices the pain, one must not credit it for much. Simply to notice the pain, though, is not the same as public processing. As long as persons experience their pain privately and in isolation, no social power is generated. That is why every regime has a law against assembly. When there is a meeting, there is social anger which generates risky, passionate social power.[6]

The following Advent, a few months after the piano crisis in 1998, Nancy Phelps, a primary leader and organizer for POP, reflected clearly and painfully in a series of writings she shared with the congregation each Sunday. It was a clear example of the public processing of grief so necessary to move forward in unity. I called her the "weeping prophet" because she cried every Sunday while reading. Here is a sample of her courageous and straightforward reflections: "I am not comfortable yet in the chasm. I thought I was, until I began to read my reflections here in church. It doesn't come easily to stand here, but at the same time I cannot ignore that to which I am called: to

---

[6] Walter Brueggemann, *Hope within History* (Atlanta: John Knox, 1987), 16–17.

keep us there until we have the real conversations that must happen. When will they happen? How will I know? I must stay here and wait."[7]

Nancy was leading us to the public processing of our grief, an important step in moving through pain to healing and hope. It was a process that continued over time through the transformation of Redeemer.

We wondered, *Who taught us that being downsized out of a career job, or not being able to pay rent, or having a nephew on drugs or in prison was dirty laundry?* We were challenging the congregation to be more real with each other. In the long run, this transformation proved to be a key for inviting new people into the community. Many are searching for authentic community, while many reject the church because they perceive it to be judgmental and hypocritical. The shift to paying attention to community proved to be vital.

> The piano story revealed a chasm between leaders and the rest of the congregation that manifested in a tie vote. More importantly, it revealed a community that was not on the same page, that didn't have deep, trusting relationships with each other.

Much later I would read and study Otto Scharmer's *Theory U.*[8] Scharmer, in academic terms, describes a descent down one side of a *U* in order to ascend the other. Transformation is not the result of walking across a bridge over problems but a collective wrestling with them into the pits of change. Figure 6.1 below builds on Scharmer's theory and provides an an image worthy of our study and contemplation as religious leaders. For us, this picture described our journey not in a path straight across linearly but in a descent down into deeper questions of identity and mission, questions we were not ready to face earlier in our history. For us, these were spiritual

---

[7] Excerpts from Advent reflections, 1998, shared by Nancy Phelps.
[8] Otto C. Scharmer, *Theory U: Leading from the Future as It Emerges* (San Francisco: Berrett-Koehler, 2009).

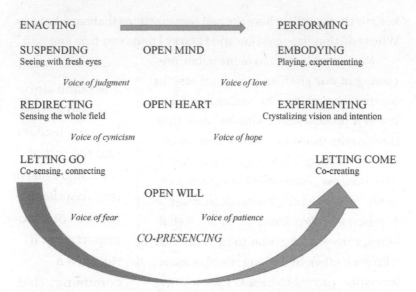

ENACTING → PERFORMING

SUSPENDING   OPEN MIND   EMBODYING
Seeing with fresh eyes   Playing, experimenting

Voice of judgment   *Voice of love*

REDIRECTING   OPEN HEART   EXPERIMENTING
Sensing the whole field   Crystalizing vision and intention

Voice of cynicism   *Voice of hope*

LETTING GO   LETTING COME
Co-sensing, connecting   Co-creating

OPEN WILL

Voice of fear   *Voice of patience*

CO-PRESENCING

FIGURE 6.1. Theory U Chart (adapted from *Theory U*, Otto Scharmer)

questions that demanded our attention and conversation. Particularly relevant was the notion of *letting go* in order to *let come*—both patient, waiting verbs.

As Redeemer moved into the chasm to build relationships, hold space for stories of grief, and focus on building community, we were learning painfully the lessons of the *U* and a powerful insight shared by Metro-IAF director Mike Gecan:

> While there may be a great deal of activity in a congregation—many committees or ministries with full schedules of meetings, events, and the like—there is often very little focused action.... As a result, most congregations never become more than the sum of their parts. Or, in the worst-case scenario, the parts of the congregation become more important than the whole. The committee, the clique, the service that you and your friends attend becomes the first priority. Any threat to that from other segments of the congregation can be met with fierce resistance and create huge resentment. The challenge for all institutions

is how to act in unison at times, so that all leaders and staff are focused on the same goal, pulling in the same direction, experiencing the same results, and evaluating together their successes and failures.[9]

A decade later, Wendy Hall, the first organizer/developer for Leaven, pointed excitedly to this section in one of our staff meetings. How might Redeemer and the newly emerging community that would become Leaven / Salt and Light "act in unison at times, so that all leaders and staff are focused on the same goal, pulling in the same direction, experiencing the same results, and evaluating together their successes and failures"? It was a question being raised already in the piano crisis, and Redeemer would have a winding road to get to the place where it was successfully embodied. Looking back, I thought of the desperate proposal I had made single-handedly in 1984 to rearrange the sanctuary. The vote then was 1–100 with a few sheepish abstentions! Now we were 19–19–19–19–19. Was this progress? What was to come of this?

As our core team became more skilled and engaged with our own members, organizing frameworks began to make sense internally for our congregational development. Our core team had connected Redeemer with the collective power of Portland Organizing Project to act on neighborhood and even citywide issues. POP also began to pay attention to building stronger institutions. Redeemer embraced this opportunity.

In June 2000, Redeemer council president Lois Jordahl and I participated in the IAF ten-day leadership training in Austin, Texas. For Lois, this was an opportunity to deepen her understanding of the arts and practices of organizing and her own skills as a leader of a congregation in transition. For me, this was my second crack at the ten-day training session, giving me an opportunity to reflect on and deepen my leadership in Redeemer, our emerging broad-based

---

[9] Gecan, *Effective Organizing*, 22.

organizing, and MACG and to pay particular attention to the congregational development aspects of organizing.

It was around this same time that I began a seven-year engagement with an ELCA Congregation-Based Organizing Team (CBOT), gathering leaders from network affiliates across the country to reflect and strategize on the roles of organizing in and for ELCA congregations. It was at one of the meetings of this group that I first heard the idea of starting a new congregation from the ground up using organizing arts and practices.

The new millennium began for Redeemer with a funeral for the church as twenty-five leaders gathered for our annual spring retreat in the sacred space of Nestucca Sanctuary. Though it was an imaginary funeral, it brought up real feelings and cemented in us that our path forward was indeed a descent. We were beginning an end, and out of the end would come a beginning. Eventually Redeemer voted to die and to trust in the resurrection, a much more earth-shattering vote than for a piano of whatever color. We were "suffering a sea-change into something rich and strange,"[10] though we did not know its shape or how to get there. Before new life would come, however, more death would haunt and threaten us and at the same time ripen us for transformation.

FOR REFLECTION

For the author, community organizing provided a vehicle to respond to pressures exerted on members and neighbors alike not by bandaging the wounded only or advocating for others but by acting directly on our own stories.

- How important is it for church leaders to identify and respond to public pressures in society?

[10] Shakespeare, *The Tempest*, act 1, sc. 2.

- What ways have you found to move from private, individual-ized Christianity to collective, community-based spirituality and action?

The red piano story is about a crisis that led to transformation.

- What crises have brought new life in your community?
- What practices have assisted your organization to move from crisis to transformation?

Compare the core team analysis and responses with the *Theory U* chart.

- What insights might *Theory U* offer you as a leader for change?

Part 3

ENGAGING THE EGYPT WITHIN

2001–2010

7 CRYING, WEEPING, WAILING

I have come down to rescue them from the Egyptians and to bring them out of that land to a good and spacious land, a land flowing with milk and honey, the region of the Canaanites, the Hittites, the Amorites, the Perizzites, the Hivites, and the Jebusites. Now the cry of the Israelites has reached Me.[1]

—Exodus 3:8–9

The courage of the seed is that once cracking, it cracks open all the way.[2]

—Mark Nepo

It had been said that death is a mirror in which all of life is reflected.[3]

—Kathleen Dowling Singh

DEATH ALL AROUND

IT WAS RASH AND INSENSITIVE OF ME EARLY IN MY TENURE AT REDEEMER to send out funeral preference forms to all the members in a newsletter. From my position as a thirty-year-old, most people in the congregation looked old to me, though many were only my parents' age, fifty and sixty. The first year I served Redeemer, I did bury eight people, and then six to eight each year for the next three decades. By the time I left, I had buried nearly two hundred beloved parishioners. I was becoming an expert at death and dying. At the same time, the

---

[1] Exodus 3:8–9, JPS H-ET.
[2] Mark Nepo, *The Book of Awakening* (Newburyport, MA: Wheeler/Weiser, 2020), 114.
[3] Kathleen Dowling Singh, *The Grace of Dying: How We Are Transformed Spiritually as We Die* (New York: HarperCollins, 2000), 5.

precarious life of Redeemer was presenting itself to us with increasing urgency. Death stalked us personally and corporately. What was it saying? How could we receive its wisdom? As a faith community grounded in the life, death, and resurrection of Jesus Christ, these should have been familiar questions. Yet up close and personal, they caused us to shiver.

The leadership shift chart[4] prepared by clergy and organizers in 1994 had become a guide as we made necessary adjustments in our congregational life. In particular, I was struck by the box titled "Tools" that listed

Reflection
Questions
One-to-ones
Tension
Death

Death?

ANGELIQUE

Even as the congregation began to come to grips with its own mortality, I experienced death firsthand. Our first granddaughter, Angelique, was stillborn on September 14, 1994. She was buried according to Yakama traditions. We participated in the Native customs as best we could, including holding back our tears until the crying ceremony. In the evening before her burial, the family, both Indian and Anglo, gathered in the living room of our daughter's aunt, which they had made into a longhouse: men on one side, women on the other, a tiny pine coffin on a woven mat in the center, and drummers on the end. Our daughter's uncle presided, at first apologizing for not knowing all the right words in his native language but then carrying on as best

---

[4] See the leadership shift chart in appendix 2.

he could. Traditionally, the drummers play seven rounds of seven songs lasting all night, with the burial itself at the break of dawn. Our daughter was just out of the hospital and still weak, however, so we did only three rounds, finishing by ten or eleven at night.

After burying Angelique at the Shaker Cemetery in the shadow of Mount Adams, we returned to the longhouse for the crying ceremony. What would this crying ceremony be? I had to wipe my eyes many times as I watched our daughter dance her grief, the drums beckoning ancient comfort and the chants lifting up primordial prayers. When the crying ceremony came, many tears had been suppressed, but others had leaked out. Who could dam the emotion welling up in our souls?

Our daughter's uncle sat us down in the makeshift longhouse and announced almost matter-of-factly that we would now have the crying ceremony. "Now we let our tears flow, for there is healing in the tears we weep. Let us share our grief as we cry together." And then he began to tell the story of the granddaughter we would never know. "Today we acknowledge that we will never hear our little sister's voice. We will never hear her cry for food or love. We will never see her sleep in our arms or hear her awaken in the night." As the first words were spoken, the room was flooded with tears. Loud wailing and quiet weeping filled the longhouse and flowed like a river.

Grief is a river. I wrote in my thesis, "I discovered that the tears were carving out a place in my heart to hold my daughter and my grief, a kind of grotto in my soul. It was both painful and comforting. In the longhouse a certain undeniable and irrevocable Hebrew spirit reminded me of my Egyptian soul, of where I had come from and where I was going. Keeping death nearby is holy work."[5] In Native American tradition, one who dies in childhood becomes an elder in the next life. Angelique is my grandmother now, among the ancestors.

> Loud wailing and quiet weeping filled the longhouse and flowed like a river.

[5] Moe, "O Healing River," 77.

"KEEP DEATH BEFORE YOU DAILY"[6]

My mom died in July 2001. Two months later, 9/11 revealed our nation's own vulnerability. As a pastor, I was immersed in death, increasingly overcome by the incessant reminders of mortality as congregation members I now had known and loved for ten and twenty years died. In a very real way, I buried the great generation.

It felt like death was all around and we were marking the death of a whole generation. We also began to grieve the death of an era as economic and cultural shifts affected our congregation. We awakened to the finitude of our bodies and peeked into the shadows of how vulnerable our corporate body was as well. Our struggle as a congregation to stay alive meant facing the threat and the opportunity that death presented.

CHANGE OR DIE

Things did need to change at Redeemer. "Change or die," as the saying goes, applies to congregations. As noted in the last chapter, we observed the rapid decline of many of Redeemer's sister congregations in Portland. Some of these congregations have revived. Many are mere skeletons of their former selves. Redeemer, too, skated with the grim reaper for over a decade, dancing on the line between vitality and further atrophy into the latter stages of death. Average worship attendance and financial wellness are considered the primary indicators of congregational health. Redeemer's worship attendance rose by about 10 percent in the first decade of its existence. The congregation experienced a rocky decline for the whole decade between 1990 and 2000. In the final decade before launching Leaven in 2013, worship attendance leveled off at fifty per Sunday. Many sister congregations in our denomination and others went through the bottom. Somehow Redeemer did not. Redeemer perched on a plateau with death very near. See table 7.1.

---

[6] *Rule of Benedict*, 4.47.

TABLE 7.1. Average worship attendance 1981–2010

Year	Attendance	Year	Attendance	Year	Attendance
1981	101	1991	93	2001	51
1982	104	1992	83	2002	53
1983	107	1993	84	2003	57
1984	116	1994	73	2004	50
1985	110	1995	70	2005	49
1986	107	1996	56	2006	50
1987	100	1997	53	2007	47
1988	101	1998	49	2008	42
1989	113	1999	48	2009	46
1990	109	2000	48	2010	49

Why didn't Redeemer fall through the bottom? Why didn't Redeemer fall into a coma as other congregations had? What kept it alive through a devastating fall in attendance? Where did the commensurate strength come from to make a transformation possible? How could a struggling congregation imagine, resource, and implement a whole new start? How did organizing and spirituality keep the body warm and the heart beating while at the same time shocking the system into a new beginning? Could death itself be our teacher and guide to another phase of life?

I asked the leaders what they thought about these questions. Nancy Phelps replied, "Somehow we had discovered hope, not wishful thinking, but a hope grounded in the deeper relationships, reflection, and prayer in which our community was engaging."

> How did organizing and spirituality keep the body warm and the heart beating while at the same time shocking the system into a new beginning?

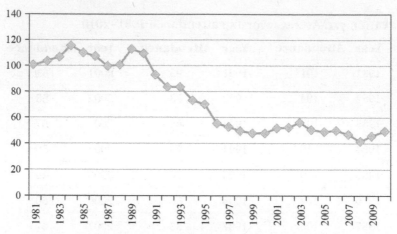

FIGURE 7.1. Average worship attendance 1981–2010

Could death be teaching us? Could death's nearness give impetus and wisdom for living? Tod Bolsinger in *Canoeing the Mountains* points insightfully to how the experience of pastors in dealing with personal death could be a resource for dealing with the death of congregations: "The same expertise pastors bring to a dying person or grieving family is what they bring to a dying congregation and grieving church family. In the same way that we help loved ones grieve the lost, remember the past and prepare to live a new life, our job as a leader is to help our community to let go and grieve so they can find a new life, a new purpose, a renewed mission again."[7]

Could we face our institutional death? Was our experience of so many deaths teaching just what Tod Bolsinger was claiming? I began to feel like our baptisms and funerals were in a race to see who would win. At Redeemer, I presided at 184 baptisms and 174 funerals. Was the difference a measure of our life? Life and death were neck and neck.

---

[7] Tod Bolsinger, *Canoeing the Mountains: Christian Leadership in Uncharted Territory* (Downers Grove, IL: IVP, 2015), 136.

A FUNERAL FOR THE CHURCH

Redeemer was facing its own mortality. For our yearly retreat in 2000, the core team planned a funeral for Redeemer. The simulated funeral began Friday night as twenty-five of us gathered in the semidark of the Nestucca yurt to introduce ourselves. It was by far the largest group to participate in any of our leadership retreats, and it included five folks who had not yet even joined the congregation. We wondered what these potential new members might think of joining a church that was having its own funeral before they joined. Leaders held their breath. Were we really going to go through with it? We were standing collectively on the precipice, staring into a great chasm between our current reality and a burgeoning vision of the fuzzy, not-yet-revealed future, a vision we could feel but not articulate. Leaders took a big risk, and the people followed.

Saturday morning, we prepared for the funeral. We remembered good old Redeemer and celebrated the gifts she had shared over the eighty years of her life. Sunday morning, we held a ceremony that included readings, hymns, a eulogy, and committal, and then we burned our written remembrances to ashes as a concluding ritual. Finally, we processed to the ocean, where our brave intern John Dummler carried the ashes into the cold, blue Pacific, casting our grief and remembrances into the great beyond.

On the way back, someone noted a nurse log near the yurt where we gathered. A nurse log is a common occurrence in forests in the Northwest. Giant fallen trees lie on their backs while new vegetation and even new giants nurse on their decaying bodies. If one looks carefully, one can see a nurse log early in its decay with the trunk still fully formed and new sprouts growing from it at all angles. The nurse log near the yurt was a small tree growing confidently from an arching dying trunk.

The nurse log became a sign of life and many years later would become a major symbol of our transformation from Redeemer to Leaven / Salt and Light. It became a major metaphor for Lenten services. It became a logo for our Living Legacy Capital Campaign,

FIGURE 7.2. Tree growing from a nurse log

FIGURE 7.3. Living Legacy Capital Campaign Logo

which raised nearly $200,000 over three years for the development of Leaven beginning in 2008.

The new vision was to come, but not that year. It was a full ten years later that the seed of the funeral and the promise of the nurse log sprouted and grew based on a three-and-a-half-year strategic plan. Ten years in the liminal space between the old and the new yielded a new vision with the capacity to move toward a new community none of us could have imagined in 2000 but all of us felt and longed for, each in our own way. Somehow this gestational space was a necessary precedent for the birth of Leaven. It was a difficult, discomforting place to be and to hold while the Spirit continued to unfold. Redeemer lay near death for a whole decade, but it didn't die before moving through a chasm to a vision and a hope. Meanwhile, we were suspended in space, where death and near death taught us valuable spiritual and organizing truths we did not want to learn.

WILDERNESS SOJOURN

Redeemer was on the cusp of transformation, but it would take time. The burning bush was white-hot yet not consumed. Having turned to it, having listened for the Spirit's voice, we were held in tense suspension, sojourning in the wilderness. The shift could not happen in haste or proceed according to our own frantic timetables. We didn't have the leadership or financial capacity to launch a major campaign of renewal, and we were trying to reinvent ourselves by ourselves. Yes, we were in relationships with other congregations in POP, but we didn't have an "other" to respond to, a relational meeting partner to ask probing questions and to bring diverse experiences. We were trying to conjure up the new from the old. We hadn't yet learned another principle from adaptive leadership—that moving through an adaptive challenge requires new stakeholders—and we were in danger of getting stuck in "the elegant tenacity of the status quo."[8]

> As we entered the new millennium, the congregation in their graves outnumbered those in the pews four to one.

We did not foresee that the way forward was a way through peril and death, just as the way for Hebrew people to escape Egypt was through the sea. Who could have foreseen the deaths we were to go through as we prepared for a new life? As we entered the new millennium, the congregation in their graves outnumbered those in the pews four to one.

BRANDON AND DIANA: DEATHS OUT OF SEQUENCE

In 2003, two deaths in particular sprang on us awkwardly out of sequence, jolting us to attention.

---

[8] Heifetz, Grashow, and Linksy, *Practice of Adaptive Leadership*, 49.

In March 2003, Brandon Scott Tobler was killed in Iraq, the first Oregonian killed in the invasion of Iraq that year. He was nineteen. A little more than a month later, Diana Lynn Owens died of pancreatic cancer at age fifty-seven. Both deaths pounded nails into our hearts and brought the reality of death near, not just at the end of long life but in its middle. Brandon died before his time in a tragic war in a far-off country. Diana died in a new stride toward healing and hope that impacted so many people and Redeemer as a whole for decades to come.

When Diana came to Redeemer, members were sharing stories from the question "How, when, and why did you come to Redeemer, and why do you stay?" Diana was clear in her response: "I had a son before I was married. I put him up for adoption but recently felt I needed to find him." Oregon had just passed new and more open rules for people involved in adoptions on all sides. "I found him. He was in San Quentin Prison and was a drug addict, but I went to see him. I'm so grateful I found him. I'm so sad he was the way he was." She continued, "Then a few months later, I heard he was released. A month later, I got a call that he had died of an overdose. He would have been thirty-four on his next birthday. That's why I'm here. I just couldn't handle the grief by myself anymore. I had grown up Lutheran but left the church out of shame when I had this first child. Now because of Nancy, I have found a community I couldn't imagine. Has the church really changed so much?"

Diana became a faithful member of the congregation and joined the core team to unearth others' stories. She worked in the federal public defender's office, often visiting immigrant and refugee detainees being held in local and county jails throughout the state. In the course of her career, she helped free over sixty individuals from many different nations. Tragically, Diana contracted pancreatic cancer shortly after coming to Redeemer. It was terminal and quick. Within nine months of the diagnosis, she died.

During the course of her illness, she chose five women to accompany her. They walked with her through every phase of her struggle. One day she and a friend went to the funeral home to make arrangements for her burial. The director was confused and asked how old her mother was when she died. Diana, forthright as ever, said, "It's not my mother. I'm making arrangements for my own burial." Her courageous journey through a blitzkrieg of cancer instilled courage and faith in all who met her. She helped unlock the fear of death for members and opened a window for Redeemer to act in faith and courage as it faced its own demise.

Our experiences of death, especially as the boundaries of personal and congregational death merged, opened us to a new imagination with an urgency we could not have manufactured on our own. The funeral for the church, Brandon's and Diana's deaths, and the multitudes in robes with palm branches who had gone before us beckoned us to step out. Mysteriously, the Spirit was teaching us through these deaths important lessons about life. We learned wisdom, courage, and the deep importance of community.

> Mysteriously, the Spirit was teaching us through these deaths important lessons about life.

GROANING, CRYING OUT, SCREAMS, CRYING

So teach us to count our days that we may gain a wise heart.[9]

In Moses's Egypt, the private pain of the many was collected into a single penetrating voice that was simultaneously a prayer to their God and an awakening to their own longing for freedom that had sunk to the bottom of their hearts, sealed away by a million bricks. "Mutely, the Israelites undergo the various torments that Pharaoh devises for them. When, finally, at the end of chapter 2, we first hear from them, inchoate cries of pain fill our ears. Four synonyms for crying are used creating an effect of crazed, wordless suffering: 'The

---

[9] Psalm 90:12 NRSV.

Israelites were groaning under the bondage and cried out. And their screams rose up to God. God heard their moaning' (Exod 2:23)."[10]

Zornberg reflects on Exodus 2:23–25 that the people's cries and God's hearing are in four parallel sets:

> The people *groan*; God *hears*.
> The people *cry out*; God *remembers*.
> The people *scream*; God *sees*.
> The people *moan*; God *knows*.[11]

She goes on to quote a nineteenth-century Chasidic writer, Mei HaShiloach (Rabbi Mordecai Yosef of Izbitza), who makes a strong connection between Israel's cries and their liberation, a close parallel to Brueggemann's concept of "public processing of pain":

> Immediately, as their cry rose up, salvation began. Till then, they had not had any arousal to cry and to pray. But since God wanted to save them, He roused in them a cry—that is the beginning of redemption. For before God wants to save, one does not see one's own lack, one is unaware of what one has not. But when God wants to save, He shows one the root of one's lack, so that one sees that all the complexity of one's needs is rooted in this basic lack. And He gives one the power of prayer, of crying out to God. One begins to rage to God about it.[12]

It is intriguing to think about how God was preparing Redeemer for its transformation. At times, we were completely unaware of what was happening. At other times, we acted consciously and with prayer, though still dragging our feet. In some small way, my experience of the crying ceremony and Redeemer's experience of the funeral

---

[10] Avivah Gottlieb Zornberg, *Moses: A Human Life* (New Haven, CT: Yale University Press, 2016), 11.

[11] Avivah Gottlieb Zornberg, *Particulars of Rapture: Reflections on Exodus* (New York: Schocken, 2001), 31.

[12] Zornberg, *Particulars of Rapture*, 33–34.

for the church—and certainly the very real roll call of deaths in the congregation and community—opened us to cry out to God in prayer and simultaneously opened God's eyes to our plight, puny as it was in comparison with Moses's people.

When did transformation begin for Redeemer? Perhaps it happened most especially when we discovered and accepted our "lack." Could it be that unearthing our individual and collective "lack" is the beginning of new life? Redeemer was lacking, and we began to know it and feel it. The deaths that surrounded us reminded us of our mortality and our inability to create a new future on our own. Like the ancient Israelites, we needed help to pass through the sea. This may be the most difficult step for many leaders and congregations to take: to feel, admit, and accept our failures, our finitude, and our lack.

> When did transformation begin for Redeemer? Perhaps it happened most especially when we discovered and accepted our "lack."

FOR REFLECTION

This chapter is an interlude, a pause to reflect back on the impact of death on ourselves and our beloved organizations. Death and grief are hard teachers, but teach they do.

- How have your experiences, reading, and reflections on death and grief affected you?
- What specific episodes impacted you most? Why?
- Who or what helped you through? And what got through to you as you journeyed?
- How have you contemplated the death of your organization?
- What is your reaction to Brueggemann's idea of "public processing of grief"?
- What insights from Zornberg agitate or excite you? Why?

8 WHO ARE WE?

Moreover, I have seen how the Egyptians oppress them. Come, therefore, I will send you to Pharaoh, and you shall free My people, the Israelites, from Egypt.[1]

—Exodus 3:9b–10

Religion is for those who are afraid of going to hell; spirituality is for those who have been there.[2]

—Ross V. of AA

Everything you do in leading adaptive change is an experiment.[3]

—*The Practice of Adaptive Leadership*

AS OUR AWARENESS OF MORTALITY INCREASED IN THE 2000S, REDEEMER found itself adrift in an uncomfortable disequilibrium. What we lacked was constantly staring us in our face. We realized that the shelf life of our existing congregation was limited, but we didn't know how to change despite reading a plethora of books and listening to experts who sometimes espoused contradictory paths forward. A part of our predicament was self-imposed. The other part was the tidal wave of a rapidly shifting world. And we knew we were not alone in this precarious place.

When the airliners crashed into the Twin Towers on September 11, 2001, little did we know the massive shift that was to unfold.

---

[1] Exodus 3:9b–10, JPS H-ET.
[2] Ernest Kurtz and Katherine Ketcham, *The Spirituality of Imperfection: Storytelling and the Search for Meaning* (New York: Bantam, 1992), 15.
[3] Heifetz, Grashow, and Linksy, *Practice of Adaptive Leadership*, 277.

Redeemer entered a long, uncertain limbo trying to stay alive when the metrics hovered at critical low points. Worship attendance had dropped to the fifties and hovered there, suspended on the thin threads of allegiance and stubborn perseverance for ten years, but we didn't drop through the bottom as many of our sister congregations did. The work of the core team and facing our own death taught us clearly one thing: whatever we did, we needed to do it together. We asked ourselves, What do you do when you don't know what to do?

DESPERATE ATTEMPTS TO GROW WITHOUT CHANGING OURSELVES

In this period, two great forces met. The past and the future clashed over Redeemer. In a way, things were cracked and yielded to a force more powerful than the "elegant tenacity of the status quo."[4] The way forward peeked through the curtains of time. Redeemer was torn open. We were at the edge of the U of transformation, but it felt like the chasm of failure, disintegration, and chaos. We were frantically trying everything in our power to keep going. Would we embrace a road less traveled or not?

Leaders tried many things to pump life into the worn corpus of Redeemer. We even embarked on a three-year process to yoke with Vernon Presbyterian, our closest neighbor and a POP partner congregation, which was groaning under similar pressures as Redeemer. We worshipped together once a quarter, then once a month, then every other week, rotating locations. Eventually, we had to decide on one location or another, and when Redeemer was chosen, Vernon membership splintered. The Presbytery seized the property and assets of the congregation. Only a fraction of Vernon members joined Redeemer, and for a time, they strengthened Redeemer. Pastor Rodgers and others remain loyal Leaven members.

During this period, we organized many experiments:

---

[4] Heifetz, Grashow, and Linksy, *Practice of Adaptive Leadership*, 49–54.

- We had parking lot fairs with music, activity booths, and a dunk tank featuring a city commissioner one year and the principal from the school across the street the next.
- A young neighbor taught a Spanish course, titled *Amigos en el Parque*, in Alberta Park across the street from Redeemer.
- Intern Kelle Nelson led the congregation out of the building to worship at various sites in the neighborhood: at a newly opened pub, McMenamins Kennedy School, at Vernon School across the street, at Alberta Park less than a block away, and at It-Is-Ness, a spiritual-not-religious storefront gathering space nearby. While this didn't attract new people like we thought it might, it did get members of the congregation out to see the neighborhood.
- We set up Alberta Park Theological Seminary, our attempt to offer classes to the broader community. Lay leaders and I taught the classes, which included the following:
  - Dreamwork
  - Science and Religion: The Message of Christ in the Modern Age
  - The Artist's Way: A Spiritual Path to Higher Creativity
  - Simplicity as Compassion: Voluntary Simplicity from a Christian Perspective

While bringing energy and enthusiasm to our members, these activities brought a few new people to the table. They were failed attempts to act our way into growth and vitality without really changing ourselves deep down.

EVALUATION AND DISCERNMENT

In a strange way, the flailing, desperate experiments that repeated activities expecting different results somehow also led to new imagination and a way forward. The key organizing practice that led Redeemer out of this swirling eddy was *evaluation*. While evaluation always happens, often in the parking lot or on the side, making evaluation an intentional part of the culture of the congregation opened the door for change. The key spiritual practice that moved us past the repetition of previous behaviors without change was *discernment.*

Our organizing training taught us the importance of evalua-tion. First, we asked leaders to identify their feelings: What were our gut reactions to activities? Sharing feelings first grounded our experience in our bodies. Feelings let our hearts speak before going to the heady work of critique. Many were not in touch with their feelings and naturally started to offer critiques from their heads. Often a leader would have to agitate the congregation by asking, "What is the feel-ing you are feeling?" Next we evaluated in two columns. In one col-umn, we asked people to suggest pluses (things that went well), and in the other column, we listed deltas (things that could change to improve the process).

> Our organizing training taught us the importance of evaluation.

Although the practice of evaluation is a key component in the organizing cycle (Listening–Planning–Acting–Evaluating), it is often skipped over. Why is evaluation often neglected? Some have had bad experiences with evaluation in other settings. It is often painful to take a critical look at ourselves in the mirror of evaluation. A good evaluation takes time, effort, and planning. It needs to be given priority in the meet-ing agenda. While we might think other things are more important, Redeemer established this practice over time, and it was beginning to pay off. We were learning to see the clashes between the past and the emerging future to which God was inviting us. We were awakening to the adaptive challenge in front of us, though we didn't have the language to describe it or the imagination or capacity to respond. What is your experience of evaluation? How has it been implemented in your con-text? What was helpful about it? What was difficult?

At the same time, Redeemer turned to the spiritual practice of discernment, something we began to do collectively. Discernment for us had a sharp edge. Its Latin root is *cernere,* "to separate, divide, distinguish."[5] Discernment is not a benign spiritual practice but leads to cutting away the old and making room for the new. This can be a painful process. Some leaders could begin to sense how the painful reflections on our current life, like Nancy's Advent reflections, were shaping a powerful tributary in the stream of transformation.

We also were becoming aware that Redeemer was not alone in facing the challenges of adaptation. The ELCA denomination as a whole began to see that the ways of the past no longer worked, and the Portland Organizing Project also began a four-year shift from a congregation-based project focused in Portland to a broad-based and metropolitan-based alliance based in the three counties of the Portland metro area.

ORGANIZING IN THE ELCA: CBOT

In 2000, I was invited by the ELCA to participate in forming a national cohort of leaders from the four major organizing networks (IAF, PICO, Gamaliel, and DART) to deepen the ELCA's investment in organizing as a vehicle for mission in the world and for congregational renewal. Previous attempts to bring the organizing networks and organizers together had exploded in turf wars and posturing. The meeting in 2000 was for organizing leaders only. Gaylord Thomas, a staff person in the Social Ministry Division of the ELCA, opened the door for this venture. Gaylord, a Black Vietnam War veteran, courageously and persistently made space for organizing leaders to meet in the ELCA headquarters in Chicago. He found funding. He staffed our meetings without laying on an institutional agenda. We named it the Congregation-Based Organizing Team (CBOT). John Heinemeier, whom I had read about in the *Christian Century* and visited in 1994, was part of the IAF component of the team and became a mentor for me.

---

[5] Rudi Laschenkohl, "Discern," Wiktionary, last modified May 2020, https://en.wiktionary.org/wiki/discern.

CBOT met twice yearly face-to-face at the ELCA headquarters, located near O'Hare Airport. Even though I lived in Portland, I could make a flight there, sit in a four-hour meeting, and fly back on the same day if necessary. In between face-to-face meetings, we caucused by phone to organize several initiatives to deepen organizing in the ELCA. During this period, CBOT organized and led three national convocations called Congregation-Based Organizing Strategic Summits. These meetings were attended by hundreds of organizing leaders, bishops, and church staff gathered to build relationships across the country, find common interests, and learn from each other. Out of these strategy summits and our collective wisdom, the CBOT began work on the following important initiatives to deepen the work of organizing in the ELCA at all levels:

- Institute a desk in the church office for congregation-based organizing. Rev. Terry Boggs, pastor of St. Matthew Lutheran, Fort Worth, Texas, and leader in the IAF affiliate there, became the first director for CBOT in the ELCA. The ELCA became the first denomination with such a position nationally. He was followed by Rev. Susan Engh in 2007.
- Work with synods to increase synodical awareness and participation in organizing. Several members of the CBOT were synod leaders. In 2007, CBOT organized and led training at the ELCA / Evangelical Lutheran Church in Canada (ELCIC) Bishops' Academy, an annual educational event for all bishops to attend. Leader/organizers were paired with network organizers to teach the main principles and practices of organizing to the bishops. I was privileged to work with Arnie Graf, a seasoned IAF organizer from the East Coast.
- Contact and engage the seminaries of the ELCA. This was an important initiative, as future pastors usually had little or no knowledge or experience with community organizing. As leaders from CBOT reached out to the eight Lutheran seminaries across the country, each one responded with some kind of course or summer offering around organizing.

- Build relationships with ELCA church leaders, especially the Division for Outreach, which included both the redevelopment of existing congregations and the planting of new ones. It was at the CBOT table that I first heard the idea of planting a church with a pastor and community organizer working together from the get-go to ground the new start in the arts and practices of organizing.
- Engage the presiding bishop of the ELCA and the bishop's office to secure increased support and funding for organizing efforts in the congregations and synods of the ELCA.

SHIFTING FROM CONGREGATION-BASED TO BROAD-BASED ORGANIZING

POP realized it was too small, too concentrated in the Portland metro area, and too exclusively made up of faith institutions, most of which were in steep decline in Oregon, to make a significant impact on big issues like housing and health care. Powerful interests locked up opportunities for affordable housing and economic equity at the state level. An example of this is the legislation passed in Salem to prohibit municipalities from enacting two ideas for increasing affordable housing: mandatory inclusionary zoning and a real estate transfer tax. POP just didn't have the power to address these issues at a state level.

After considerable debate and lengthy discernment, POP decided to disorganize and reorganize, to build a larger, metropolitan broad-based organization on the bones of POP. "Metropolitan" meant Multnomah, Washington, and Clackamas Counties and included Portland and major suburbs adjacent. "Broad-based" meant opening the organization from only Christian congregations to include other religious groups—Jews and Muslims, at least—as well as labor unions, school organizations, and community-based nonprofits that shared an interest in the common good. A four-year process of inviting new organizations, building relationships, figuring out how to work together, and agreeing on action items culminated in the founding assembly of the Metropolitan Alliance for Common Good on May 23, 2002. The *Northwest Labor Press* reported, "Sitting in blocs 12 abreast, nearly 1,500 participants—many of them union members—packed a hall at the Oregon Convention Center for the May 23 founding assembly of a new labor-community coalition: the MACG. The group is the product of years of discussions among leaders from churches, unions and community organizations. Participating institutions intend to work together on four issue areas: Access to health care; sustainable work and development (emphasizing conservation and union-wage jobs); affordable housing; and public education."[6]

It was an exciting day, as over forty organizations formed "an organization of organizations" for the common good. Over half were faith-based organizations, including five Lutheran congregations and Jewish, Muslim, and Unitarian communities as well. One-fourth of the room was made up of delegates from labor, mostly the building trades, whose primary interest was the development of green jobs. It was a proud day, like the rainbow day at Redeemer, discussed in chapter 5.

OPENING TO THE WORLD

Organizing also taught us that one-to-one meetings were vital as we crossed many institutional boundaries and learned cultural protocols. I recall a model one-to-one during a teaching session with Ben Nelson, a young organizer for the Laborer's International Union. I learned he had majored in political science at Willamette University, which is near the Oregon State Capitol, but when it came time to do an internship, he didn't want to become a legislative aide as many of his peers had done. His advisor asked if he would be interested in working with the American Federation of Labor and Congress of Industrial Organizations (AFL-CIO), also with offices near the capitol.

---

[6] *Northwest Labor Press*, June 7, 2002.

"What's the AFL-CIO?" he had asked the advisor. I was shocked. It never occurred to me that he had fallen into labor, followed by a formation process. He had his own burning bush experience in his own way. Then it occurred to me that we shared an important connection. I had fallen into the church world, and it totally shaped my life. He had fallen into the labor world, with parallel ramifications. I was learning the complexity of the worlds that made up the one world in which we all lived. Bit by bit, I learned about the Black world, the Indian world, the world of women pastors, and the labor world, to name just some. I learned that one-to-ones connect not just individuals but, in a very real way, whole worlds.

In my organizing work, I met plumbers, imams, high school principals, food workers, teachers, and an ex-con whose dream was to build a community reentry process using the arts and practices of organizing, a dream that is unfolding as Phoenix Rising Transitions. All these worlds came together in organizing. That, for me, was and is spiritual. As I and others met people outside of Redeemer through organizing, we also began to attract new people to our congregation. Somehow Redeemer had become a gateway for the most interesting people to come and sometimes stay, people who seemed to appear out of nowhere, arriving with a big, blank story cloud above their heads like a package unopened.

> All these worlds came together in organizing. That, for me, was and is spiritual.

Scott, who started out as our musician/choir leader and eventually went on to lead a major organizing and outreach process, came to Redeemer, it seemed, out of the blue. He was not a church musician but a composer, a gig master who had classically trained at the San Francisco Conservatory of Music. He adapted easily and learned the liturgics, led the choir, and even played the organ a little to please the elders. He was likable, smart, and talented.

Unbeknownst to us, however, he was a fifteen-year heroin addict. He lost his day job. He started asking for advances on his meager church salary. He even started sleeping at the church. One day in September 2002, the church treasurer reported to me that Scott had forged and cashed checks from our account, totaling about $600.

What to do?

Our organizing and spiritual instincts kicked in. We made a plan to invite him into a process of repentance and restitution. Because Scott had participated in many prayer circles as a listener, we hoped he would be open to such an approach for himself. Our council president, who himself had participated in many prayer circles, including a life-changing one for him, made the call:

1. We fired him and asked for the church key back.
2. We offered him forgiveness without any strings attached.
3. We invited him to come back and join a yet-to-be-determined process of reconciliation, including paying the congregation back the money he had stolen.
4. We invited him into recovery, something he began to talk about, including previous attempts at treatment followed by relapses, a pattern we learned was so common.

Then we waited. What were the odds that he would take us up on our request and meet with us face-to-face? 100–1? To his credit, he did. He offered his key. He expressed his shame and guilt and accepted our face-to-face forgiveness. At the same time, the legal system offered him jail or treatment. He chose treatment. We made one-to-ones with him; I met with him almost every week, others as they could. We kept him close.

ENTERBEING

Even while our participation in community organizing was bearing fruit, Redeemer was a creaking Lutheran ship sailing into a postmodern world with tattered sails. Others around us were beginning to respond to the new world unfolding. One intern gave us a taste of a new congregation formed in Minnesota in a garage with its slogan "The Church with the Big Open Doors." The creative pastor of a Hood River congregation opened a storefront ministry called Soul Café near the windsurfer part of town. It consisted of coffee, dialogue, and reflection for the "spiritual, nonreligious." Our organizing core team was shifting from outside work to internal development.

Our reading and experience with those who identified as spiritual but not religious led us to invest in an off-site spiritual outreach. In the summer of 2004, we convened a team of mostly young leaders loosely connected with Redeemer: Sam Phelps, a sixteen-year-old high school student and son of a key Redeemer family; Carrie Hatha-way, a twentysomething eclectic granddaughter of Joan Lepley, then council president of Redeemer and ELCA pastor; Eileen Gebbie, gay, tattooed, eclectic daughter of a solid suburban Lutheran congrega-tion, St. Luke in Southwest Portland; our current intern, Ori Pauley; Ali Ippolito, an extraordinarily talented musician; and Scott, a bit older and freshly steeped in recovery wisdom. It was a fragile and formidable team. In Advent 2003, we launched the first series of Wednesday-evening gatherings at a local art/spiritual spot called CoreSource with a theme for each night. The area, which was the size of a large living room, was set up with candlelight and cushions on the floor, a contrast from the pews and stained glass of Redeemer. Poetry was read and Taizé music sung. The themes for the consecu-tive weeks were relax, release, receive, and rejoice.

I began to identify Scott as a potential leader. One day, Scott came flying into my office: "Pastor Moe, Pastor Moe, I found my Bible!" "You what?" I replied. "I found my Bible. It talks about base-ball." I knew Scott loved the Detroit Tigers, but I still didn't get the connection with the Bible. "You know, in baseball, if someone hits three hundred, they're a star. That means they fail seventy percent of the time!" Then he showed me the book tucked away in the crook of his arm: *The Spirituality of Imperfection*. I ordered myself a copy and read it cover to cover. Soon Scott and I were co-leading a group in the Redeemer chapel on the spirituality of imperfection. We taught a couple of rounds, Scott reaching out to the recovery community and I to the church side. Then he co-led a new group with another lay leader. Over the next year, the spirituality of imperfection found its way into sermons, core team meetings, and retreats. One leader suggested we rename our church "Less Than Perfect Lutheran Church."

We invested in Scott's development. We sent him to the IAF ten-day leadership training in Chicago and to a two-year spiritual direction program run by Sister Antoinette, my spiritual director, at Shalom Prayer Center in Mount Angel. Scott ate them both up. Spirituality and organizing struck chords deep in his heart. He called it "Recovery Phase II."

In the months that followed, I grew more and more fond of Scott. He lost some of his bullshit. He became more honest with himself and with us. He came to the council for forgiveness, as a step toward reconciliation. In April 2004, he told his story to the whole congregation and was received back as a member in good standing. In June, he completed his court-mandated treatment program. In August 2004, we offered him a new job as the director for a satellite ministry that eventually became known as "Enterbeing," a new word they made up from the verb *enter* and the noun coined by Thich Nhat Hanh, "interbeing," the concept that no being is single, but we "inter-are" in a relationship.

Enterbeing moved out of Redeemer into a studio apartment just six blocks from Redeemer on Alberta Street, a street that in 1988 was part of a crack cocaine epidemic and in 1998 began a slow swing toward a kind of recovery of its own, with art studios and coffee shops beginning to break through the boarded-up buildings and cracked sidewalks. Roslyn's Garden Coffee Shop, where I found the red piano, was nearby.

For nearly six years, Enterbeing rented this one-room apartment with a partial kitchen, a restroom, a storeroom, and six hundred square feet of open space with large windows facing a now bustling Alberta Street. We received funding from the ELCA and the Oregon Synod as well as a partner congregation, St. Luke in Southwest Portland. Vernon Presbyterian and Redeemer, now working in partnership, invited member contributions to Enterbeing in addition to their regular offerings. And leaders passed the hat at Enterbeing to help make ends meet. It was lean, but it worked.

There were many bumps and bruises, but Scott came from behind the curtain, so to speak, and out onto the stage of Redeemer, of Enterbeing, of organizing and recovery, and he made such a difference in inviting others from their hiding places, including those of us hiding in the confines of Redeemer as it was or as we wanted it to be. Scott taught us much from his own recovery, and *The Spirituality of Imperfection* became a textbook for our outreach efforts: "Viewing religion, 'the spiritual' see rigidity; viewing spirituality, 'the religious' see sloppiness. Religion connotes boundaries, while spirituality's borders seem haphazard and ill defined. The vocabulary of religion emphasizes the solid; the language of spirituality suggests the fluid."[7]

Enterbeing also hosted a new artist each month for the "Last Thursday on Alberta" art displays. It hosted a Thanksgiving dinner each fall. Classes for Redeemer and community folks expanded to include the following:

- "Experiencing the Heart of Christianity," based on the book by Marcus Borg
- "The Soul of Money," based on the book by Lynne Twist
- "Engaged Spirituality: Thich Nhat Hanh and Thomas Merton," taught by me and Buddhist leader Peggy Lindquist; over the next years, Peggy and I taught Buddhist/Christian perspectives, including Joanna Macy, Thomas Berry, and others
- "Strapped, Stretched, and Stained," exploring the pressures on our households
- "B.S.* You Won't Hear in Church *(Bible Studies)"
- "From Wild Man to Wise Man," based on the book by Richard Rohr

---

[7] Kurtz and Ketcham, *Spirituality of Imperfection*, 23.

The heart of Enterbeing, however, was the Wednesday-evening gatherings, which grew out of our experiments in spirituality and organizing. Wednesday gatherings met regularly from 7:00 to 8:30 p.m. and were attended by people from both Redeemer and the community. Scott, Ali, and others figured out a weekly pattern:

Inviting the Bell
Opening Meditation Music
Introduction of the Theme and Storyteller
A Reading Chosen by the Storyteller
Story (10–12 minutes, related to a monthly theme)
One-to-Ones (How does the story told impact you in your
    own journey?)
Collective Reflection
Song
Passing the Hat
Closing with Candles

The circle attracted an array of various and sundry folks who told their stories and reflected on the stories of others in a mix of spiritual and nonreligious readings and songs and a closing with candle prayers. The number of Redeemer members who attended grew. At first, most came to support the outreach, but they increasingly returned as they recognized the value of this open-source spiritual gathering. Rob Wentzien, Redeemer's congregational president in 2006, wrote insightfully and prophetically about Enterbeing:

When Enterbeing began its ministry on Alberta three years ago, I hoped it would be a place for people to begin exploring their spirituality and then decide to become a member of a traditional church. We hoped Enterbeing would be a place new members to Redeemer would come from. However, since its inception I've come to look at Enterbeing's relationship to Redeemer in a different way. Instead of Enterbeing being the place for people to enter Redeemer and participate in the traditional model of being church, it is a place for people like myself who grew up in that model to learn how to be the church in the 21st century.[8]

Rob had suffered from a terrible seizure disorder but had recently gotten enough relief to get married and to reengage his calling to ordained ministry. He had given up on becoming ordained decades before because of his illness. With his seizures more under control, he completed ministry candidacy requirements, including a brief internship at Redeemer, before assuming a call in Shishmaref, Alaska, a remote island community near the Arctic Circle. He served nineteen months with his loving wife, Muriel. One evening, while home on leave from his work in Alaska, he suffered a seizure outside Enterbeing, something he had experienced a hundred times before. This time, he fell backward and crashed to the sidewalk. He fell into a coma and died a couple of days later. Before he died, however, Redeemer members flocked into his intensive care room to read, pray, and touch this beloved man.

MY OWN DISCERNMENT

On a personal level, I entered my fifties during this period. Our children were grown and gone, and our daughter, who was still living on the Yakama Indian Reservation, had another child, our second grandchild, in 2003. My wife, Michelle, as a result of her accompaniment of Diana Owens through her dying, became a hospice nurse after working in the Oregon Burn Center at Emanuel Hospital for twenty years. I continued to value my monthly visits with Sister Antoinette, who turned seventy-five as I turned fifty and who, despite a year of cancer, was vibrant, sharp, and wise.

[8] Rob Wentzien, *Redeemer Lutheran Church Annual Report*, 2006.

I felt a call to learn Spanish, as the Latinx population was the fastest-growing minority group in Oregon. I tried several classes. I listened to tapes. I wrote in notebooks. Eventually, I signed up for a program in Cuernavaca, Mexico, where I stayed with a multigenerational family. Each day, I rode the bus to the school in another part of town, and on weekends, they took me on excursions to meet people and see the sights.

On my fifty-third birthday, I was in Cuernavaca again, writing a prayer for discernment. Should I stay at Redeemer or seek something else? I knew that my age could become a factor for congregations choosing me as a pastor. I also realized that I wanted at least ten years in whatever new call I might find. My prayer was simple: "If it wouldn't be too much to ask, could you, God, please send me a sign about my future by the time I'm fifty-five?" In my own naive way, I thought giving the Spirit two whole years was plenty of lead time.

My fifty-fifth birthday came and went without fanfare. I had had a couple of nibbles for job opportunities, but nothing substantial. So much for my discernment plan! The next month, however, Dick Harmon, now the regional director for IAF Northwest, and Joe Chrastil, the lead organizer in Spokane, Washington, invited me to be part of the organizing staff to build a new broad-based organization in Seattle, Tacoma, and surrounding communities in King and Pierce Counties in Washington State. It was a juicy proposal that I seriously considered.

Three months after my birthday, I made a four-day Jesuit discernment retreat. I was using the time of discernment to determine whether to stay at Redeemer or to move to Seattle to become an organizer in what would become Sound Alliance, named for the cities around Puget Sound. My spiritual director for the retreat encouraged me to pretend I had decided one way or the other and then to write about how it felt. I chose organizing, and it felt good. It was exciting. I was jazzed. I even wrote a letter to the congregation outlining my intention to move on. I never sent the letter. I wanted to be both a pastor and an organizer. I consulted with John Heinemeier, a mentor pastor deeply engaged with organizing on the East Coast and a leader on the ELCA CBOT. He asked, "How much of your identity on a scale of one to ten is being a pastor?"

I said, "I'm about a seven or an eight."

"That's pretty high," he replied.

Over the summer, the air went out of my discernment balloon. My enthusiasm for becoming an organizer in the Seattle area began to wane. Michelle and I had driven up north to look at housing. We were set back by the cost and busyness of this new terrain. Michelle would have to change jobs. I looked back to Redeemer but with fresh energy, since I knew I had options.

At this very time, a small window was opening for Redeemer. I noticed a commercial property for sale for $1 million on the burgeoning Alberta Street, which was just five blocks from Redeemer. Redeemer owned a similarly sized plot on the west side of the church that was an unused parking lot and a rental house we leased to a food pantry. I wondered if the congregation would consider selling some of its property in order to fund significant outreach. I thought the property might be worth at least half the Alberta Street property. I consulted my best friend from high school, a real estate appraiser in Portland who thought we could sell each lot in our parcel for about $100,000. We had six lots in the parcel I was eyeing. I shared my research on this question with key members of the council. Next we met with property experts whom we had met through our work in POP and MACG. Everyone we consulted agreed that some development of the property was feasible and could yield what my appraiser friend had guesstimated. I began to wonder if it might be possible to build a new community on the site of the old Redeemer. This was an exciting new opportunity that the council was open to exploring.

FOR REFLECTION

Some of Pastor Moe's mentors encouraged experimentation and failure as the best teachers. A good idea from a distance, but up close, too hot to handle!

- What risks have you taken? What failures have you endured?
- What prevents you from taking risks? What opens you to risking for the sake of new life?
- What experiments have led to great learning and even transformation?

Pastor Moe was fortunate to have a congregation open, really broken open by trying and failing a lot. It takes courage and imagination to learn.

- What are the key elements for you to build a learning organization?
- How have you learned to fail and to learn from these failures safely?
- What more do you need?

9 CONFRONTING THE EGYPT WITHIN

But Moses said to God, "Who am I that I should go to Pharaoh and free the Israelites from Egypt?"[1]

—Exodus 3:11

Who are we? What does God want us to do? How can we be faithful to God's call?[2]

—Diana Butler Bass

It is the congregation's ecclesial imagination that over time gives rise to the pastor's pastoral imagination. It is the congregation's ecclesial intelligence that is the source for the pastor's intelligence.[3]

—Craig Dykstra

AS I TURNED IN MY DISCERNMENT BACK TO REDEEMER, IT WAS CLEAR THAT I could let go of old Redeemer and invest fully in whatever transformation was unfolding, even if it meant the death of what was. The congregation's vote to sell some of its property was a sign that it too was looking ahead and not back.

Digesting the deaths of a whole generation of saints would have been enough, but Redeemer was also dealing with its own nearing-death experience. In 2007, I drew a diagram that portrayed a response to the decline we were experiencing. I was presenting our leadership

---

[1] Exodus 3:11, JPS H-ET.
[2] Diana Butler Bass, *Christianity for the Rest of Us: How the Neighborhood Church Is Transforming the Faith* (New York: HarperOne, 2007), 91.
[3] Craig Dykstra, "A Way of Seeing: Imagination and the Pastoral Life," *Christian Century* 125, no. 7 (2008): 30.

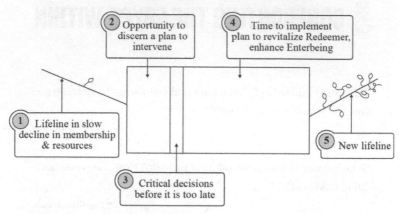

FIGURE 9.1. Lifeline diagram

with a time-critical, urgent, yet strategic opportunity: make major shifts now while we have resources and capacity or continue the decline until it's too late to respond. Redeemer responded.

LEADING BY PROPOSAL, RESPONSE, PROPOSAL AGAIN

A *proposal* in organizing terms is a clear statement of possibility given to an individual or group to consider. I tried to make proposals out of deep listening but also at the edge of where people were and where the Spirit was leading. At the confluence of Spirit and people's receptiveness, movement becomes possible. I made many proposals in my tenure at Redeemer, often with the core team's input and discernment. Some of these proposals were scrapped, but more often they were reworked and relationalized and became sturdy banks for the river of newness to flow through. Too many directions, too many activities, too many different proposals make for a shallow, meandering stream. We needed a deep river of prayer, conversation, and conviction. In December 2007, the congregation adopted what we called the "Bold and Modest Proposal." Though this proposal was never fulfilled, it provided an agitation and an imagination that prompted greater flow and clarity in the next phases. The Bold and Modest Proposal laid out the following:

- a three-year campaign to increase Redeemer's capacity to invite and welcome others and deepen ourselves and others in a bold and faithful response to God's amazing grace
- a goal of $1 million for capital and outreach investments from property sales, churchwide funds, and a capital campaign
- an intention to call an associate pastor for outreach
- specific building improvements, including accessible restrooms, energy-efficient windows, and new lighting

> I was presenting our leadership with a time-critical, urgent, yet strategic opportunity: make major shifts now while we have resources and capacity or continue the decline until it's too late to respond.

Many of these things were accomplished. Some were not. The importance of the proposal was that it got concrete steps out in the community for conversation and discernment. Together we came up with a clear and concise statement that guided us into the future.

A LARGER, MORE MIXED AND POWERFUL SPIRITUAL COMMUNITY

Soon we discerned a more precise and focused vision: "to build a larger, more mixed and powerful spiritual community with and alongside Redeemer."

Surely Proverbs speaks wisdom in the often-quoted King James Version when it says, "Where there is no vision, the people perish."[4]

---

4 Proverbs 29:18 KJV.

This is most certainly true. However, a corollary is equally substantial: without people (capacity, money, leadership), the vision perishes!

How could the stars and planets line up for Redeemer to make a way where there was none? Who could foresee a path out of failed experiments to a future and a hope? Why didn't discouragement and despair torpedo any attempts at a working vision? Could prayer and organizing empower a shift of the magnitude necessary? Could the emerging vision be powerful enough to overcome perils unknown? Would money become an insurmountable obstacle? These questions taunted us and also drove us to collective discernment. Discernment is both an organizing and a spiritual practice, twisting the strands of these two tributaries into a powerful river rolling toward an unknown future, but a future with a hope. Author Dorothy Bass puts it this way: "It is easy to understand discernment as an individual process, but in the study congregations, discernment was also a corporate process. The churches learned to ask questions of God, then listen carefully to God's inner wisdom for the community. Who are we? What does God want us to do? How can we be faithful to God's call?"[5]

POWER BEFORE PROGRAM

Before organizing what was to become Leaven / Salt and Light, leaders of Redeemer faced a crucial obstacle: how to raise enough money to pay for the dismantling of Redeemer and the building of something new. Long before we dreamed of a makeover (little did we know it would become a total replacement!), I had resolved in my mind never to let money be the reason not to do something that needed doing. This proved helpful in establishing the intern program and Enterbeing, among other projects. It was an important mindset that not everyone shared, but a growing number began to see its wisdom. I had also learned the wisdom of IAF's hard-nosed policy that leaders need to raise three years' funding before it would

---

[5] Bass, *Christianity for the Rest of Us*, 91.

build a new organization in a community. I knew that a traditional mission-pastor approach was insufficient. To give a new community a chance, we needed three years' funding—and three years for a pastor and organizer to work together on the new mission while the congregation continued alongside the project. That raised the critical question, How could we more than double our income for a long enough period of time for something new to take root while keeping the mother ship afloat as well? In organizing, we had learned "power before program." Or as Jesus says in Luke, "For which of you, intending to build a tower, does not first sit down and estimate the cost, to see whether he has enough to complete it? Otherwise, when he has laid a foundation and is not able to finish, all who see it will begin to ridicule him, saying, 'This fellow began to build and was not able to finish.'"[6]

The first task of organizing this larger, more mixed spiritual community was an action we needed to take: raise enough money to pay two and a half additional salaries for three years and keep it sequestered for that purpose only. That total alone was nearly a million dollars!

We had also learned in organizing how to break down a problem into manageable pieces, a series of actions geared toward a single large goal. In this case, we broke the money into manageable pieces:

1. By 2005, property in our neighborhood was rising sharply. We owned six lots in our residential neighborhood, including an unused parking lot and a small house, about 20,000 square feet in all. We appointed a property research and development team. We soon learned that our back six lots were worth up to $600,000. The congregation had already approved selling these back six lots "to fund significant outreach and to do something good for the community," presumably affordable housing.

2. While the team worked at selling the property, we appointed another team, the living legacy team, to develop a capital

campaign not for improvements but to add to the mission fund. The thinking behind this was twofold. First, we knew that the money from the property alone would not be sufficient. Second, we knew that there had to be buy-in from the existing congregation members. Would members draw from their IRAs, pensions, property sales, or other assets to fund a vision still forming? People's real commitment needed to be demonstrated. We hired a consultant who worked with us to raise about $200,000 over three years (2008–10) in what we named the Living Legacy Fund.

3. Simultaneously, we approached the Oregon Synod and the ELCA mission department for additional funds, eventually piecing together about $200,000 over the three years of the building of Leaven / Salt and Light.

This was the plan that worked its way through the formal and informal decision-making processes at Redeemer, a miracle in and of itself. As plans go, it was a good plan. And as plans sometimes go, it didn't go as planned.

PLANNING THE WORK AND WORKING THE PLAN

At first, the property team steamrollered along. It began work in the summer of 2005, and by October of 2006, we had a full-price cash offer for the six lots we had agreed to sell. The offer came from a reputable nonprofit community development corporation, Home Ownership One Street at a Time (HOST). HOST planned to build eighteen to twenty units of lower-cost (60–80 percent of median income) housing on the lots we sold and to pay us $660,000! We felt like we had died and gone to heaven. This sale met our standard criteria for doing something good for the community and funding significant outreach in the community.

However, during the due-diligence process with the city, we were informed that we would have to renew our conditional use permit, a city requirement for nonprofits existing in residential neighborhoods. Whenever a significant change of use is indicated, a whole review process is reopened. Selling a mostly unused parking lot, in this case, triggered the conditional use process because the sales potentially affected neighborhood parking. This also allowed the city to tack on other updates, such as a sewer inspection. We didn't know what it meant at the time, but soon we learned that we would need our own attorney. At the end of the day, we had spent eighteen months in the process and spent over $30,000 we didn't have. We had spent $15,000 on our attorney's fees and $15,000 on city fees, plus other funds needed to make necessary physical improvements such as parking-lot drainage, street access, and a new fence. This was money we did not budget or have on hand. We had to borrow money from the Oregon Synod to pay these costs. This was only the beginning of many obstacles. Some view obstacles as a sign that you are moving in the wrong direction; it must not be God's will. Redeemer's leadership took a different view. Vi Webb, the Finnish *sisu* woman, encouraged us: "These obstacles are signs that we are on the right track!" Really? More obstacles came. More time passed. How long, O Lord?

By the time we had completed the conditional-use permit process, the housing development landscape had changed. The 2007 "housing bubble" had burst. Foreclosures outnumbered home sales. Stingy banks became even stingier, denying many loan applications as housing costs fell. Even though these big banks had received a $700 billion bailout from the government in 2008, they continued to invest in Wall Street rather than neighborhoods. For Redeemer, this crisis threatened the fragile plans of a small-time player in an unfathomable global economic shift. The land sale was on hold. First the community-based nonprofit lowered its bid to $500,000. Later they withdrew that offer as well. Six months later, it was out of business and bankrupt, a victim of housing-investment policies made in inaccessible, distant boardrooms. Would our plan also lie on the Jericho road, beaten by robbers and left to die?

> We regrouped. We had come too far to turn around now.

No. We regrouped. We had come too far to turn around now. Somehow the heat and light of the burning bush still burned.

PRAYERS OF THE PEOPLE

One of the ways we regrouped was to turn to prayer. Redeemer was used to prayers being read from a book in liturgy. Gradually, members became more open to spontaneous prayer. Intern Solveig Nilsen-Goodin had introduced Redeemer to "candle prayers," lighting a candle and placing it in the sand with or without words. Other invitations to pray came in retreats and over time were added to liturgy.

Redeemer wasn't used to extemporaneous prayer, so we often invited folks to first write their prayers on cards and then offer them out loud. Some of the prayers written were included in notes and newsletters. These prayers were read in liturgy. I became aware of how prayerful the people were becoming and how prayer was transforming each of us.

Here are some prayers from December 2005:

Creator and Master Builder: give us open minds to see the direction you would like us to go. Help us discern the needs and opportunities in our community.

May we as a community be willing to stay and stand in the tension of this project, as well as other tensions, so that our faithful God might fully use us to God's glory.

Lord, I pray that we can find a way to keep our church.

Please help us proceed thoughtfully and generously.

The years of waiting and hoping tempered our prayers. Notice the shift in tone in these prayers from December 2007:

I pray for the courage to walk the path and accept God's mission as my own, even when I don't see the outcome.

I pray that this process of discernment be the spark that lights a holy fire in the life of Redeemer/Enterbeing.

Lord of all life and hope, fill us with the power of your spirit. Give us hope for today and tomorrow and beyond. Show us the ministry you choose for us.

Lord, we ask that you give us wisdom, boldness, energy.

These prayers from the hearts of the people echo one from *Lutheran Book of Worship* that became a mainstay through the difficult discernments and actions Redeemer was negotiating. We often prayed it responsively, and after a while, many memorized it: "Lord God, you have called your servants to ventures of which we cannot see the ending, by paths as yet untrodden, through perils unknown. Give us faith to go forth with good courage, not knowing where we go, but only that your hand is leading us and your love supporting us, through Jesus Christ our Lord."[7]

MAKING A WAY

The dream for me was to fund a pastor and an organizer over a three-year period to transform Redeemer. This imagination came from the CBOT, which gathered Lutheran leaders from community-organizing efforts across the country. It arose from a what-if: What if new congregations were developed using community-organizing wisdom and practices? It was a new idea to me but stuck in my mind. For years I had been intentional about introducing interns at

[7] *Lutheran Book of Worship* (Minneapolis: Augsburg Fortress, 1978), 153.

Redeemer to community organizing. Now I was looking for talent to fulfill this vision. Though we had no secure funding, we negotiated a call with a talented former intern, Melissa Reed, to come to Redeemer on a part-time call as an associate pastor beginning in November 2008. In order to pay for her call, I assumed a part-time position as interim director for MACG. Basically, I became part-time pastor for Redeemer and half-time interim director for MACG. In turn, Melissa became part-time pastor for outreach at Redeemer. In November 2008, Melissa was ordained at Redeemer and called to a one-year call as associate pastor for outreach. We hoped this would turn into something more full-time, but the vision was fuzzy, and the funds were precarious. The property sale was stalled. The Living Legacy Fund was just beginning.

SUSTAINABLE WORKS[8]

My work in MACG led me into an interesting long-term project to connect multiple interests around energy. *Sustainability* was becoming a buzzword in the political world as the first serious considerations of the impacts of global climate change followed Al Gore's 2006 documentary, *An Inconvenient Truth*. Those concerned with the environment were calling for reductions in greenhouse gas emissions. Others, especially those in organized labor, wondered if a new green economy might offer living-wage jobs for those in the trades. And many people across the board were being affected by rising energy costs. How might these disparate interests lead to a unifying action?

A strategic summit of organizing staff and leaders from Washington and Oregon gathered to wrestle with what we were hearing and what opportunities might be lifted. A staff person from the City of Portland Office of Sustainability brought valuable information and vision. We learned a lot about conserving energy. This connected

---

[8] See appendix 4 for more about Sustainable Works, from MACG, December 2008.

with our members' interests in reducing rising energy costs as well as saving the planet.

Existing residences accounted for 40 percent of greenhouse gas emissions. With deep energy retrofits (insulation, efficiency furnace replacements, duct sealing, etc.), emissions could be reduced up to 50 percent. This would provide good local jobs. If mandated city- or statewide, it would make significant reductions in emissions, and due to the efficiencies created, people would use less energy, thus reducing their monthly costs. If such a project could be subsidized, homeowners could see reductions even while paying back the cost of the retrofits. It was a triple-win proposal!

Because Washington had two affiliates, one in the Seattle/Tacoma area and another in Spokane, and because it had significant labor membership involved in retrofit work, sheet metal, plumbers, pipe fitters, electricians, and insulators, Washington took the lead in the project. The Washington IAF Northwest affiliates worked to provide subsidies for this work legislatively and statewide and then created a nonprofit entity, Sustainable Works (SW), to actually do some of the work in both Spokane and in the Seattle/Tacoma area. I served on the SW board for five years as SW implemented an aggressive plan to pay fair wages, reduce emissions, and save money on consumers' energy bills. In Oregon the situation was more complex, as unions refused to join MACG, and we had only one base in Oregon, Portland metro. Soon a city entity, Clean Energy Works, initiated sustainability work in Portland, but without the emphasis on labor standards or any effort to reduce energy costs for consumers. The project skimmed off the top for those most interested and capable of paying for retrofits with little concern for working-class folks or widespread participation. MACG stepped into this void and contracted with the city to make a hundred retrofits in the modest neighborhood of Cully, just a mile east of Redeemer. This project did have strong labor standards and was committed to retrofits for low- and modest-income families. It was called Changing the Climate in Cully. Although it was successful, it didn't prevent most of the benefits of energy retrofits floating up to the higher-income neighborhoods.

Sustainable Works in Washington, however, expanded to make thousands of retrofits in Spokane and Seattle, Tacoma, and Federal Way between the two. Sustainable Works built a tight organization of over fifty employees earning living wages and invested in the new green economy. Some of this was made possible by stimulus funds from the government, which IAF affiliates had worked to secure through state legislation. Soon, however, private companies entered the fray, lowered labor standards, and ignored needs in poorer neighborhoods. This allowed them to make retrofits for less, thus undercutting SW. After five years, Sustainable Works went out of business. It was a great effort, but faced with the vagaries of open competition without labor and utility standards, Sustainable Works just couldn't compete.

In a way, the Redeemer property sale and funding plan faced similar obstacles; affordable housing had become less available as large banks and investment companies commodified housing, bundling home mortgages and trading them on Wall Street. This kind of speculation artificially inflated housing costs and made it difficult to own a home, especially for first-time home buyers. For developers, it was not cost effective to build more modestly priced housing when they could make more money building higher-end homes. Realtors, too, benefited from higher-cost homes, as their commissions were a percentage of the sales price. Why make $12,000 on a $200,000 home when one could make twice that on a $400,000 one with the same amount of work? The market had definitely shifted from the first home we bought in Portland for $60,000 at 14 percent interest. Costs spiraled upward in Portland and elsewhere across the country. For Redeemer, the affordable housing portion of our vision became less and less doable. We adjusted our plan, swallowed our idealism, and took the affordable housing portion of the vision off the table. We would sell the lots at market rate and count on the community outreach to fulfill our goal of doing good.

This proved easier said than done. While developers were still eager for work, banks and other lending entities were not loaning for local development. Finding a developer who could generate their own funding became nearly impossible. Finally, at the end of 2009, we were in fruitful negotiations with a local developer who had cobbled together private financing to buy and develop two of our six lots. He was offering $190,000 for the two lots. In the meantime, Redeemer was running on fumes. We had taken out a $25,000 loan from the synod to pay for the conditional-use permit process. Pastor Reed was on a one-year call that we renewed month to month, not knowing when or how we could call her to more. This was extremely stressful for all, especially for Pastor Reed and her family.

> Leadership agitated the congregation to make critical decisions before the money came in. This was a stretch. This was an act of faith.

Leadership agitated the congregation to make critical decisions before the money came in. This was a stretch. This was an act of faith. In 2009 Redeemer held seven official congregational meetings to make decisions, each preceded by one-to-ones, small-group forums, and large gatherings of the whole community, Redeemer members and newcomers, brought to the table by Pastor Reed. It was awkward because at the congregational meetings, only Redeemer members could vote. Some newcomers joined the congregation officially, but many did not. The team did the best it could to include these new voices, holding many open conversations and having straw votes that included all before the official votes were made.

By the grace of God, all seven congregational votes, unlike the contentious red-piano vote, were overwhelmingly positive—29–2, 32–3, and so on—on various funding options. This included a December resolution on funding and staffing with the understanding that this plan would begin as soon as the property sold so we wouldn't have to revisit it after the money came in.

In January 2010, the first two properties sold. In February 2010, Pastor Reed, Wendy Hall, Scott Brazieal, and Ali Ippolito began their work on the new mission, soon to become Leaven Project, eventually to evolve into Leaven Community / Salt and Light Lutheran Church.

On January 22, 2010, a check for $148,976 was presented to the new mission from the sale of the property ($190,000 minus the costs of the sale and synod loan repayment). The new mission was launched February 1, 2010. Our musician, Ali Ippolito, drew a large check from the bank of the ancestors to present to the congregation:

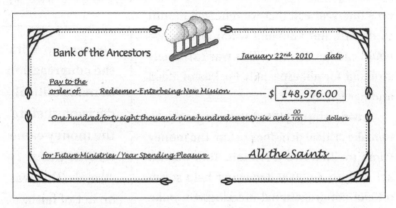

FIGURE 9.2. Check for new mission

With this symbolic check, we were connecting the new mission with the investment of those who had gone before us. This was not just a property sale; it was a gift from the ancestors to continue a legacy.

"A SPIRAL OF MUTUAL INFLUENCE, ENCOURAGEMENT, AND EMPOWERMENT"

What was going on for me as pastor at this time? How was I thinking about the next phase? What were my worries? What hopes were coming to light?

It took me a long time to rely on others, to turn over the ministry of the congregation to a leadership rather than trying to steer them according to my own instincts and seminary training, valuable as these were. A shared experience of organizing and spirituality moved us to great imagination and courage, beyond any one of us. A collective discernment and determination emerged. Craig Dykstra, in an article written in 2008, captures this movement beautifully:

> A spiral of mutual influence, encouragement, and empowerment takes hold when pastors and congregations give these gifts of God to and receive them from one another. Pastoral imagination is a gift that is given by God in and through communities of faith possessed of deep, rich ecclesial imaginations. Ecclesial imagination is a gift that is given by God through the sustained nurture and shaping ministry of wise and faithful pastors with deep, rich pastoral imaginations. Through eyes of faith, pastors come to see the abundance that is before them and that surrounds them already. Through eyes of faith, they can see what gifts they have been given in the people, who, however flawed, are the members of their congregations. Likewise, through eyes of faith, the members of congregations come to see the abundance that is before them and surrounding them too. And through those eyes, they can recognize what gifts they have been given in the people who, however flawed, have become their pastors.[9]

Prayer and organizing now flowed into one another, forming a powerful river that both destroyed the existing contours of community that had served in their time and, in one flow, opened a way for new vision and energy to spring forth. Letting go was yielding to letting come.

FOR REFLECTION

This chapter probes the difficulty of changing our minds and acting differently.

[9] Dykstra, "A Way of Seeing," 31.

- How and in what ways have you become aware of your limitations?
- How have you conceived and acted on your own liberation individually and collectively?

Reflect on Dykstra's idea of the "spiral of mutual influence."

- When, where, and how have you experienced such a spiral, such synergy?
- How can your leadership move you and your organization toward more of this?

Part 4

MAKING A WAY THROUGH THE WILDERNESS

2010–2013

10 WALKING INTO THE WILDERNESS

And He said, "I will be with you; that shall be your sign that it was I who sent you. And when you have freed the people from Egypt, you shall worship God at this mountain."[1]

—Exodus 3:12

When we are experimenting with new solutions within a living system, we are doing so with something that has a history, is alive and precious, and must be handled with care.[2]

—Tod Bolsinger

And no one puts new wine into old wineskins; otherwise the new wine will burst the skins and will be spilled, and the skins will be destroyed. But new wine must be put into fresh wineskins.[3]

—Luke 5:37–38

THE OLD AND NEW CLASH OVER REDEEMER'S DESK

A BISHOP IN THE OREGON/WASHINGTON REGION ONCE QUIPPED, "THE OLD and the new clash over my desk!" And the old and the new were clashing over steeples, altars, pulpits, and council tables all over the church.

The day Pastor Reed came into my office to say, "I don't think it's working. We just can't put new wine in old wineskins," I felt my world wobble on its axis. We had to look at things differently and create a new plan. How could we dislodge our previous ways of thinking?

---

[1] Exodus 3:12, JPS H-ET.
[2] Bolsinger, *Canoeing the Mountains*, 107.
[3] Luke 5:37–38 NRSV.

Could we break out of our brick building, our unrevised constitution, the ways of life that for the past ninety years had been in place? These things were no longer working, and many we were working to change already. More startling for me was the realization that I was part of the problem. I realized that if I was to be part of the solution, I needed to come to grips with how I was part of the problem as well. The old and new were colliding over Redeemer.

Redeemer's core team shifted to understand its role as discerning the critical questions the community needed to engage in together. The complexity of this discernment made a quantum shift as we figured out how to include new voices at the table. New teams needed to be built.

Since shifting to the strategy of starting a new mission alongside Redeemer, I felt like I was skating backward, accelerating, watching the past and present fading further and further in the distance while trying to look over my shoulder to see where we were headed. I couldn't see. I couldn't imagine. I couldn't fathom the new, even though my gut told me to keep going. Pastor Reed, Wendy Hall, Ali Ippolito, and the newly emerging community, the new wine, were so beautiful, so promising, so dedicated and talented. I rested in their hope.

Nancy Phelps, Dick Harmon, John Rodgers, Bea Gilmore, LaVeta Gilmore Jones, Lois Jordahl, Joe and Debbie Morgan, and so many others from the old Redeemer were turning to skate forward into the future, not fully envisioning or understanding what was to be but trusting that something rich and strange was emerging from the nurse log we were. The new community that was emerging was eager to skate forward, ready to lead.

OFF TO THE RACES: ONE STEP AT A TIME

Once the first property sold, the new mission soon to be christened "Leaven Project" bolted out of the gate. All had been put in place. In December, we were ready! In January, we were on our marks! The property sale in January was the starting gun. In February, the staff team was off and running.

We began weekly staff meetings. We read books together, debriefed our one-to-ones, and strategized the next steps. In March, we went away for a two-day retreat. Pastor Reed, Wendy Hall, Scott Brazieal, Ali Ippolito, and I had already worked together in Enterbeing. But this was different. This was new territory for all of us. This was not tweaking the old into something better. This was a teardown and replacement. This was putting the new first and letting the old drop. The vision that had evolved in the work of Enterbeing and Pastor Reed's outreach was crisp, clean, and challenging, as Leaven's first annual report stated:

> On February 1, 2010 Redeemer Lutheran Church, in partnership with the Oregon Synod and the ELCA, started the, later named, Leaven Project with a vision to build a larger, more powerful, more diverse (race, culture, sexual orientation and gender identity, age) spiritual community with and alongside Redeemer-Enterbeing that
>
> • honors the experience, creativity, and imagination of all generations;
> • relates, listens, and acts through spiritual practice and the telling of stories;
> • is rooted in the Lutheran tradition of grace and justice while embracing complementary spiritual expressions;
> • responds to cultural, economic, and ecological inequity through the arts and practices of organizing.[4]

TEAMS

The key to the next period was teamwork. Or, I should say, *teams*work, as a variety of teams were organized, reorganized, and/or dissolved as new phases emerged. We had already developed a culture of teams

---

[4] *Redeemer Lutheran Church Annual Report*, January 2011.

in the last phase of our process. Throughout the three-and-a-half-year project, we created teams of all kinds, each strategically discerned for balance, strength, and compatibility. These teams needed to be parsed among existing Redeemer members and new leaders emerging.

At the staff level, we set goals for one-to-ones and created the "Proposal for Action in First 100 Days of the New Mission." We were grounding the new effort in relational work. This was an important DNA to bring from organizing into the new community. From hundreds of one-to-ones, staff would come to understand what mattered most to people and at the same time assess the interest and potential of new leaders. Key questions guided these conversations:

1. What kind of spiritual community would bring you life? Why?
2. What of your spiritual upbringing continues to be helpful in your life?
3. What of your spiritual upbringing needs to be shed?
4. What new elements of spiritual formation might be helpful in the new mission?

These were the questions we began to ask among ourselves in one-to-one meetings. What we chose to ask was not generic or formulaic. What we ended up with was not what we envisioned at the beginning. Next, an emerging core leader team of five leaders, all from Redeemer, joined the staff in listening. This new team organized house meetings at Enterbeing to bring people from Redeemer and new folks together. In April, forty people gathered for discernment and relationship building as a result of the work of the staff and core leader team. Members of Redeemer and new folks in mixed small groups gathered around two primary questions distilled from the many one-to-one meetings:

What are the pressures on you and your loved ones?
What would be a relevant spiritual community for you?

This was classic relational organizing, which the staff and initial core team had already been practicing at Redeemer—some for many years. Now it was about a dramatic new undertaking. We had set foot in new territory. We were, in Tod Bolsinger's terms, "going off the map."[5]

THE FIRST LEAVEN ASSEMBLY: MAY 23, 2010

And again [Jesus] said, "To what should I compare the kingdom of God? It is like yeast that a woman took and mixed in with three measures of flour until all of it was leavened."[6]

At the launching assembly of Leaven Project on May 23, 2010, Oregon bishop David Brauer-Rieke commissioned the new organizing staff and commended Redeemer for living out our theology of death and resurrection.

In addition to meeting with people individually and gathering small groups, Leaven Project created many activities to bring people together in other ways:

- Bras, Bible, and Brew gathered women from a cross-section of the community.
- Enterbeing opened space in Wednesday gatherings for new and existing leaders to share their visions and questions.
- Organizing the Bio Commons set a table for people to organize in the face of global climate disruption.
- An initial local action formed as people were organized to move their money from corporate banks that had betrayed local communities into a member-owned credit union, Advantis.
- A community garden sprouted in Redeemer's front yard.

---

[5] Bolsinger, *Canoeing the Mountains*, 15. See also chapters 7–11 of Bolsinger's book.
[6] Luke 13:20–21 NRSV.

- New leaders attended weeklong IAF leadership training and local MACG leadership institutes.

The action to move money from corporate banks to a member-owned credit is a good example of how Leaven exercised the organizing cycle (listening, planning, acting, evaluating) to move to action based on people's values and interests. In the listening season, leaders heard story after story of student debt, escalating housing and rental costs, and rising health care costs. At the same time, the big banks were being bailed out by federal intervention. What could be done?

The idea of credit unions has a long history. Some trace their origins to a priest in Canada, Rev. Dr. Moses Coady.[7] Credit unions sprang up in church basements and union halls and became popular alternatives to banks. Leaven leaders researched local credit unions and then organized households to move their money from their bank to Advantis Credit Union as a collective action. This is important. Collective action. Leaven could have recommended using credit unions and left it up to individuals to make a choice. Rather, Leaven organized groups of ten and twenty to move their money together at the same time in a single action. Moving money from banks to the credit union as a group demonstrated the power of collective action.

By moving a large number of accounts to Advantis, the people demonstrated the power to negotiate with Advantis around a variety of economic pressures. Could Advantis offer better student loan rates? Would Advantis supply loans for households engaging in a residential energy retrofit pilot project being organized by MACG? Could Advantis help struggling families with a "shared secure lending pool," a low-interest loan program secured by Leaven members' collateral? Since credit unions are member-based organizations, the possibilities seemed endless. Advantis at the time had about forty thousand members, with several branches in the Portland area. It was a medium-sized credit union, but research had shown that it

---

[7] For Moses Coady, see the Coady International Institute, St. Francis Xavier University, https://coady.stfx.ca/moses-coady/.

was strong fiscally. Over time, some sixty households from Leaven and allies moved their money to Advantis. Leaven leaders attended the annual meeting of Advantis to get a sense of the internal workings of the credit union and to meet people. While Leaven leaders gathered near the entrance to the meeting, the CEO of Advantis walked by, noticed the group, and came over. "You must be Leaven," he said as he introduced himself. Indeed.

Michelle and I happily moved our money. Leaven was able to flex its own muscles and to learn from this action. I felt this financial action could have become a MACG-wide issue, garnering the power of more institutions to negotiate on housing and equity issues already being researched, but I wasn't directly involved in this leadership and chose to not push this agenda.

A NEW LEAVEN CORE TEAM

In July 2010, a whole new Leaven core leader team was in place. This time six of the ten members were new, not existing Redeemer members. A July retreat proposed new goals:

1. Review and learn from the first five months of organizing.
2. Look forward to the next six months, set goals, and make timelines through December 2010.
3. Discuss and come to agreement on the organizing principles for the next period.
4. Develop an asset map[8] that included Redeemer, Enterbeing, ELCA, Oregon Synod, and Leaven Project.
5. Relax, reflect, and have some fun!

---

[8] I was first introduced to asset mapping at one of the denominational social ministry conferences by John McKnight, who went on to develop the Asset-Based Community Development Institute (ABCD) at DePaul University. ABCD approaches problems and issues from the strengths of a community rather than identifying the needs and trying to address those.

Later in July 2010, Melissa and Wendy participated in ELCA mission-developer training in Minneapolis. Soon after this, they engaged in the ELCA Mission Cohort, led by Rev. Susan Engh. The cohort, an important new initiative of the ELCA congregation-based organizing office, brought together organizing leaders from across the country dedicated to using organizing to start new congregations or redevelop existing ones.

In the following six months, leaders organized difficult conversations as visions and expectations were clarified and some hard decisions were made. After prayerful discernment, we closed Enterbeing in September 2010, ending a nearly six-year experiment. A rent increase was part of it, but leaders also felt that Enterbeing had served its purpose and that all our effort had to go into Leaven. We were learning that sometimes things have to end. In a way, this situation was just a practice run for the eventual closing of Redeemer so that Leaven / Salt and Light could thrive.

As the calendar turned to 2011, things were looking promising. A well-attended Leaven retreat in February 2011 brought together existing leaders from Redeemer and new emerging leaders from Leaven. Though it was a Leaven retreat, Redeemer members participated. While it included familiar one-to-one meetings and storytelling, it also included dance parties during breaks and a consensus-style decision-making process. The old and new were clashing over Leaven/Redeemer. Two wall sheets from gatherings tell some of the story. The first asked leaders to reflect on the meaning of the congregation and Leaven Project so far. The second asked for what was most important or essential going forward and what might be given up. The lists below are from the responses at the meetings taken down on wall sheets and transcribed:

What is the meaning of Redeemer / Leaven Project?

- birth of future, intergenerational
- spiritual needs of current community and children be met
- Redeemer meaningful, but noticing more young people

- sharing ideas
- turning, branching out
- recovery
- garden action
- worship smaller, need cross-pollination
- unchurched find both valuable
- great legacy of saints
- old ones can be useful

> After prayerful discernment, we closed Enterbeing in September 2010, ending a nearly six-year experiment.

At the same time, tensions were beginning to rise around finances and leadership. The plan to sell the six lots of Redeemer stalled after the first sale of just two lots in January 2010. The money from that sale was rapidly depleting. The second property was still in limbo, though we were negotiating with the same developer to purchase the second parcel as well. More importantly, leadership faced a difficult structural issue. Redeemer was the only legal entity formed with council and congregational structures. Redeemer members were therefore the only ones who could vote on

TABLE 10.1. Essential versus give up to survive

Essential	Give up
Consensus process	Current congregation/council is not essential
Openness, willing to experiment, take risks	Fear-based thinking
Relational culture, stories, build trust	Pastor structure, legalistic, bureaucratic
Public accountability	Deficit/survival mode
Personal, institutional storytelling	Avoidance of difficult issues
Evaluation, reorganizing	Building/structure as it is
Spiritual literacy, live out the gospel in practice	

critical issues of finances, new structures, leadership, and so forth. Plus, the new Leaven leaders didn't want to just follow Redeemer's practice with Robert's Rules of Order and hierarchical authorities. Leaven wanted to be a consensus organization that provided opportunities for everyone to participate and have a say in what happened. How were these necessary tensions to be negotiated? Clearly part of the solution was relational.

We began referring to ourselves as "Redeemer/Leaven," which recognized both parts in the newly emerging organization. On the other hand, the slash was a sign of difference, even division. Could this transitional title threaten our unity and puncture the objective of building a new community? Were we dividing ourselves with a slash? And worse, could it widen into a chasm, as Redeemer had experienced following the red-piano vote?

Our reading and reflection as staff and leader teams were hardly keeping up with our experience. In this case, however, Dorothy Bass, in her helpful book *Christianity after Religion: The End of Church and the Birth of a New Spiritual Awakening*, was spot on:

> Human beings rarely move toward the future without the fear of loss or the fear of risk. . . . Anxiety is frequently the mark of personal transformation, for anxiety is the primary emotion when the heart feels disoriented and lost. Indeed, awakenings and the backlash they spawn may not happen with great regularity, but when they do happen to individuals and societies, great tension and division is a normal (if disconcerting) part of the process of spiritual and cultural revitalization. In this situation, leaders and spiritual communities are not needed to comfort people feeling lost in times of change. Instead, spiritual leaders need to help transform these fears into urgency and courage.[9]

---

[9] Bass, *Christianity after Religion*, 250–51.

Interestingly, the academic literature was moving along similar lines as Leaven. We wove in and out of several important books together as a staff, sometimes sharing excerpts with teams and/or the whole community during gatherings. The following were some of the important books we read and discussed:[10]

- *Gracious Space: Working Better Together* by Patricia Hughes (2004)
- *The Soul of Money: Reclaiming the Wealth of Our Inner Resources* by Lynne Twist (2006)
- *Signs of Emergence: A Vision for Church That Is Organic/Networked/ Decentralized/Bottom-Up/Communal/Flexible (Always Evolving)* by Kester Brewin (2007)
- *Effective Organizing for Congregational Renewal* by Michael Gecan (2008)
- *The Practice of Adaptive Leadership: Tools and Tactics for Changing Your Organization and the World* by Ron Heifetz and others (2009)

While none of these books alone proved to be the whole answer, each added incrementally to our understanding. More importantly, each increased our confidence and courage to continue. We were moving into an uncomfortable period of necessary disequilibrium. It was a complex journey through the unknown for both Redeemer and the emerging leadership of Leaven. For Redeemer, it brought feelings of loss and grief. On the Leaven side, many felt impatience and anxiety. It was just plain uncomfortable.

A big question loomed: How could old leaders figure out a way to give authority to new Leaven leaders to dream new dreams and plan new visions when Redeemer still held the ultimate authority for major decisions?

For Leaven leaders tooled in organizing, this was a power question with no simple answer. What Redeemer gave, Redeemer could

---

[10] For more detail, see the bibliography.

take away. We were not simply starting a new Lutheran congregation in place of the old Redeemer. Rather, the vision laid out and agreed upon was *to build a larger and more mixed spiritual community with and alongside Redeemer*. The Leaven vision included one of community that

- honors the experience, creativity, and imagination of all generations;
- relates, listens, and acts through spiritual practice and the telling of stories;
- is rooted in the Lutheran tradition of grace and justice while embracing complementary spiritual expressions; and
- responds to cultural, economic, and ecological inequity through the arts and practices of organizing.

Some of the new folks coming to Leaven were not interested in joining a church or becoming Lutheran. Leaven was a spiritual community, not a Lutheran church. On the other hand, Redeemer was a Lutheran congregation, and it was turning itself over to something only vaguely spiritual. How could these tensions lead to newness and not to conflict and fragmentation? How would all the variant voices be authentically heard in the new mix coming together?

Fortunately, once again, our decades of organizing experience had groomed us in the art of compromise, in polarizing and depolarizing, in seeking a third way, a win-win rather than a win-lose scenario. Our growing ability to deal with the tensions we had confronted in negotiating with city hall and powerful developers was put to the test. We were learning that new things are often born out of such tensions. As Ron Heifetz astutely points out, there is a "productive zone of disequilibrium"[11] that is necessary to make change. However, if tensions reach an intolerable point, the process can shut down in a hurry. As leaders, we were learning to monitor this productive zone in a Goldilocks manner: not too hot, not too

---

[11] Heifetz, Grashow, and Linksy, *Practice of Adaptive Leadership*, 28–31.

cold, but just right. Of course, that's a judgment call that requires careful discernment.

The answer that evolved over time was twofold:

1. Deep relationships of trust and understanding needed to be cultivated across the old and new communities. This called for ongoing relational work in the organizing sense, something Redeemer had been practicing for a decade or more.
2. A new format for making decisions needed to be forged that prioritized some form of consensus discernment.

A major element in this phase was the development of community gatherings that included both existing Redeemer members and Leaven folks. These gatherings were co-led by existing Redeemer and emerging Leaven leaders. This modeled for people the changes happening in our midst. Once again, our experience in organizing many meetings and practicing one-to-ones was invaluable. At every meeting, people were given opportunities to listen and tell their stories and build relationships. Sometimes a new person and an existing Redeemer member would make a one-to-one in front of the whole group, talking candidly about their backgrounds, hopes, and dreams. Without this relational organizing approach, Leaven would never have gotten out of the gate.

> A major element in this phase was the development of community gatherings that included both existing Redeemer members and Leaven folks.

A second important element in the process was to experiment with consensus decision-making. Fortunately, Leaven found help in Tasha Harmon, an organizational consultant. Some decisions could be made by consensus by just calling the question and getting a sense of the room. At other times, leaders asked for straw votes. Sometimes color-coded cards were used for voting, as leaders got more sophisticated with the process. Green was 100 percent go; yellow was go with caution; orange was strong reservations; red was a no go. Everyone got to show their colors. When orange or red cards came up, leaders listened to those holding them. These votes, especially if they concerned money or structural questions, were not binding. At times official congregational votes had to be taken with only Redeemer members voting after the straw votes. It was clumsy, but usually the Redeemer vote mirrored the larger community vote. Eventually, the clumsiness became more streamlined.

All this had to be worked out by the Leaven teams in regular premeetings to plan the agenda and adjust on the fly. The practice of premeetings and appointing rotating cochairs is a key practice of organizing that allows the process to move forward with input and buy-in from the whole team while guided by a leader team. Some processes get bogged down because the leadership gets ahead of the membership, and then they are surprised that everybody doesn't see it the same way. The red-piano saga is a painful example. While this approach initially takes more time and effort, in the long run, it is the only way we could move forward. Inch by inch, with the leader teams formulating proposals and vetting them at gatherings, so many eyes could begin to shape the vision, and many views could be considered as the whole emerged.

Gradually, a picture of our new community began to emerge. Eventually, at one of the gatherings, a leader from one of the tables went to the wall sheets and drew a diagram of the "One New Community" she envisioned. Someone from another table exclaimed, "That looks like a peanut!" And everybody laughed, but the name stuck (see figure 10.1, top diagram).

At subsequent gatherings, another diagram was presented that was more complete (see figure 10.1, bottom diagram). These pictures helped the community move. Words that described the movement followed:

> The new entity is One Community, a non-profit membership organization, within which is an ELCA congregation. Everyone

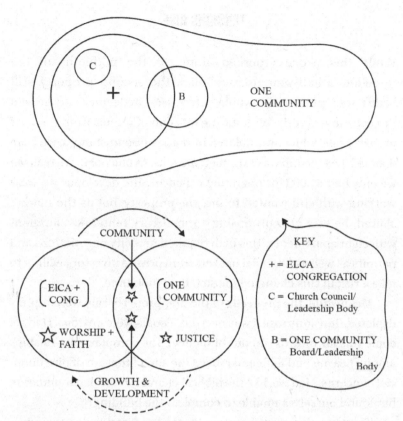

FIGURE 10.1. "The Peanut" diagrams

is a member of the non-profit; those who choose are members
of the congregation as well. All members of the congregation
are members of the One Community.

The structure of the One Community's governance gives
equal voice to the entire community. The general structure
is that we are One Community with a board to oversee the
community living out its vision and mission. We also have an
ELCA congregation within the One Community that contains
a council to oversee all ELCA and congregational matters.[12]

---

[12] Leaven report at July 31, 2011, congregational meeting.

TENSIONS RISE

While this process perked along, at the midpoint of the three-and-a-half-year mission plan, the second property still hadn't sold, putting the whole enterprise—Redeemer and Leaven Project—in jeopardy. Without the infusion of money from the next property sale, which was delayed by market circumstances, we were doomed. Leadership was extremely anxious. At one point, we realized we only had $1,000 for operating expenses. The developer we were working with still wanted to buy the property, but as the market shifted, he was now proposing a three-story rental development with eight apartments. This plan required new city negotiations and permits as well as financial backers from private investors willing to take a risk in this changing market. It all took time.

Meanwhile, the proceeds of the first property sale were rapidly depleted. Tensions rose. I was nervous. People were anxious. Had we come this far only to run out of money? The complex relationships among Leaven and Redeemer faced the added tension of dire financial concerns. Had we, like the biblical characters, built a foundation but found ourselves unable to complete the building?[13]

Tensions also arose between Pastor Reed and me as the funds sank lower and lower. She had risked the most. I could retire and lick my wounds, but she had a family to support, and transitioning rapidly to a different call would be a hardship. Besides, we were both invested fully in this dream. Two things helped us break through the tension. First, we agreed to get help from Consultation to Clergy, the regional counseling arm of the Lutheran Church. Second, we explored ways to relieve the financial pressure until we finalized the property sale that we believed was imminent.

What could we do? We had already borrowed money twice from the Oregon Synod in $25,000 increments. We had also borrowed money from individuals in the congregation, called debenture loans, informal notes indicating Redeemer's intention to pay the notes

[13] Luke 14:28–30 NRSV.

back when the property sold. During this time, one person even proposed that we consider planting a St. Joseph statue on the property. (At the time, realtors were buying plastic saints by the gross, and sellers were burying them upside down in their yards all over.) It was a stretch for our spirituality, and to my knowledge, we never actually did it. That it came up at a community conversation was a sign of our desperation and a down-to-earth prayer for selling the second parcel. Secretly, I think someone did bury a St. Joseph on our property. Who knows?

As leaders pored over the numbers and examined and reexamined the budgets, we discovered some dedicated funds buried (a St. Joseph?) in the assets of Redeemer—an outreach endowment of about $11,000 and a scholarship fund of about $60,000. What better way to spend the endowment for outreach? What good would either do if the whole ship went down? Redeemer council voted to liquidate both funds and made a proposal to the congregation at a special congregational meeting in July 2011. The vote was near unanimous: Redeemer was all in.

This relieved the immediate financial pressure, but the leadership issue was vexing as well. Behind closed doors, Pastor Reed and I began a serious conversation about the transition from Redeemer to Leaven and the new, yet-to-be-named ELCA mission congregation. It was a difficult conversation. We made a wise choice to consult with the Consultation to Clergy counselor, Rev. Phil Streufert, located in Seattle but serving the six synods of region 1. We only had two sessions with him. In the course of the conversation, we happened on a what-if (thank you, Holy Spirit!): What if we proposed an eighteen-month plan for Redeemer/Leaven from January 2012 through the founding of Leaven in June 2013? The core of the plan included the following:

- Phase 1, January–June 30, 2012: Pastor Moe will announce at the 2012 annual meeting his plan to retire from Redeemer in June 2013. Pastor Reed and Pastor Moe continue to work together for six months.

- Phase 2, July 1–December 31, 2012: Pastor Moe will go on sabbatical with time to develop Transformational Leadership for IAF Northwest; Pastor Reed will take over as full-time lead pastor for Redeemer and Leaven during sabbatical.
- Phase 3, January 1–June 30, 2013: Pastor Moe will return from sabbatical part-time at Redeemer and part-time as IAF Northwest director for Transformational Leadership; Pastor Reed will continue full-time as lead pastor and mission developer for Leaven and the new congregation.

The congregation accepted the plan. Having a plan mitigated much of the anxiety of the transition process for both of us. Pastor Reed embraced the path to stronger leadership of Leaven; I was able to devote some of my energy to applying the lessons I was learning to other congregations and organizations.

The second property sold in November 2012, making a way for the unfolding of Leaven. The third and final property didn't sell until after I left. The property plan we hatched in 2009 didn't work out as it was laid out, but it did yield $600,000 over the four-year period, providing more than half the funding necessary for the development of Leaven.

FOR REFLECTION

Planning the work and working the plan is an adage that holds a challenging truth. Good planning without implementation is worthless, and, of course, any plan needs effective follow-through to make it successful.

- What are the key components for you of a good plan?
- What are the key components of working the plan?

Bringing new leaders into the mix can be a challenge.

- How have you negotiated the mix of new and existing leaders in your organization?
- What have you learned about how to do this?

Building consensus to move forward is a key component of successful change. This often involves negotiating the tension of competing ideas, personalities, and emotional energies.

- What tensions have you negotiated?
- What components or practices made it possible to move through tension to consensus?

11 MAKING A WAY IN THE WILDERNESS

Moses said to God, "When I come to the Israelites and say to them, 'The God of your fathers has sent me to you,' and they ask me, 'What is His name?' what shall I say to them?" And God said to Moses, "Ehyeh-Asher-Ehyeh." He continued, "Thus you shall say to the Israelites, 'Ehyeh sent me to you.'"[1]

—Exodus 3:13–14

All organizing is dis-organizing and re-organizing.[2]

—Michael Gecan

You are the salt of the earth; but if salt has lost its taste, how can its saltiness be restored? It is no longer good for anything, but is thrown out and trampled under foot. You are the light of the world. A city built on a hill cannot be hid.[3]

—Matthew 5:13–14

IN NOVEMBER 2021, THE SECOND PARCEL OF PROPERTY FINALLY SOLD FOR $165,000, securing the next years of Leaven's development. The third and final property didn't sell until after I left in June 2013. Eventually, however, the portion of funding from property sales reached about $600,000, the amount projected in 2008. The sale took a lot longer than we planned! I turned to skate forward into my new calling with IAF Northwest as director for Transformational Leadership, building on the experience and learning in my years

---

[1] Exodus 3:13–14, JPS H-ET.
[2] Gecan, *Effective Organizing*, 5.
[3] Matthew 5:13–14 NRSV.

at Redeemer and with organizing. Leaven was now out in front, and I knew I couldn't keep up. It was time for me to back off, time for Leaven to lead. We had a plan. We set a target date. This target date laser-focused our energy on founding the new community in eighteen months: June 30, 2013.

Grounded in a long history of organizing and spiritual exploration, Leaven now stood tall in the woods. But before the founding assembly happened and concurrent with its planning, the work of transformation accelerated. The first six months of the eighteen-month plan flew by. Most of the work shifted now to the Leaven Project staff and leaders. My role remained mostly with Redeemer to assure a smooth transition and add what wisdom I could.

Pastor Reed really thrived during this period as she took on more and more responsibility for the whole of Redeemer/Leaven. Wendy Hall Curtis was also developing into a top-notch leader and organizer. Wendy and Pastor Reed were different in their approaches and roles but communicated well and complemented one another beautifully. Their primary work was to put life into the vision of a new community, one that had never been imagined or built before. It was complex. How could a new member-based nonprofit organization and a new ELCA Lutheran congregation partner in a mutually beneficial manner? It had many moving parts. How could this chaos be organized to move together? The answer was teams, transitional teams, and more teams. Transitional teams eventually became more permanent elements of the new entity coming into being, working creatively and diligently toward the vision laid out. They often adjusted and revised but never compromised. And a new, more detailed structure was presented that included many new teams plus the existing Redeemer council and their correlations:

> How could a new member-based nonprofit organization and a new ELCA Lutheran congregation partner in a mutually beneficial manner?

ONE COMMUNITY (INTERIM) STRUCTURE

The new proposed structure was meant to serve until Leaven got its own 501c3, at which time the "assembly" will be made up of all Leaven members who all have an equal vote in the community.

- interim organizing team (IOT): programs, outreach, membership and leadership development, messaging, and PR
- interim development team (TDT 2): financial capacity, legal/ structural, budget planning, transition planning
- council (Redeemer Lutheran's board): elected by Redeemer members; delegated to oversee use of funds, mission, bylaws, and articles of incorporation of Redeemer Lutheran Church (of which Leaven Project is currently a project)
- assembly (eventually includes community, neighborhood groups, and Redeemer Lutheran): ultimate voting authority up to and until Leaven Project gets its own 501c3 status with the IRS; in relationship with and part of Leaven Project leadership
- interim coordination team (ICT): coordinates among all the teams, Redeemer's council, and the emerging assembly

The first two years of organizing one step at a time included hundred-day plans, countless one-to-ones, early-morning strategy sessions, retreats, regular gatherings, and intentional discovering and cultivating of many leaders. But now the planning sped to a gallop as the finish line and new starting gate beckoned in the distance. While the pace increased, new muscles were being flexed and developed. Working through tensions between Pastor Reed and me and among leaders from Redeemer and the new emerging Leaven Community put new sinews and synergy into the body we were building. More importantly, the new organization was not to be a flimsy grassroots organization whose tufts could be pulled out by the roots, or mowed over, or stomped into the ground but one grounded in the long legacy of congregations and other institutions that had roots and branches. No, the new organization needed to be built to last, like trees deeply rooted and strong, as the psalmist and Isaiah proclaim,

> They are like trees
>   planted by streams of water,
> which yield their fruit in its season,
>   and their leaves do not wither.
> In all that they do, they prosper.[4]

> They will be called oaks of righteousness,
>   the planting of the Lord, to display his glory.
> They shall build up the ancient ruins,
>   they shall raise up the former devastations;
> they shall repair the ruined cities,
>   the devastations of many generations.[5]

Pastor Reed reported on this period in her 2012 annual report: "After 23 months together as Redeemer and Leaven Project—discovering one another and our shared mission, learning from one another's stories, and discerning our future together—we enter the next 18 months of transition and integration that promises transformation. Our Phase I Transition Discernment Team led us through a diligent process of strategic planning, producing foundation for our founding as one, new, transformed community in May of 2013 that includes a non-profit membership-based organization and an ELCA worshiping mission congregation, as well as a road map to our development, growth, and founding."[6]

During this critical period, leaders had to write formal documents for the new Leaven nonprofit and the new ELCA mission congregation, Salt and Light. Nothing like this had ever, to our

---

[4] Psalm 1:3 NRSV.
[5] Isaiah 61:3b–4 NRSV.
[6] Pastor Melissa Reed, "Leaven Project 2011-2012-2013: Transition, Integration, Transformation," *Redeemer Lutheran Church Annual Report*, 2012.

knowledge, been proposed, so we were breaking new ground. The old saying I heard a hundred times in negotiations between POP or MACG and corporate or government entities came back to our court: "The devil's in the details!" While I agreed to some extent, I also came to believe another maxim: "The angels are in the details." Leaven leaders, with the assistance of Tasha Harmon and expert legal advice, accomplished the hard work of drafting, editing, and making proposals to the larger community to gather input to further modify the documents. The whole community ratified a final draft ready to be submitted to the ELCA for approval.

A "HERE WE STAND" MOMENT AT ELCA CHURCHWIDE

In July 2012, Pastor Reed and Bishop Dave Brauer-Rieke flew to ELCA headquarters in Chicago to meet with the secretary of the denomination and ELCA attorneys to share the story of Leaven and to gain approval for the preliminary documents. The support of Bishop Dave was crucial, though Pastor Reed's articulate, passionate, and persuasive eloquence needed no backup. Once again, the careful development of relationships with leaders in the ELCA proved invaluable. The support of Rev. Stephen Bouman, director for congregational and synodical mission; Rev. Ruben Duran, who headed the division responsible for new mission congregations; and Rev. Susan Engh, director for congregation-based organizing, was invaluable.

Pastor Reed and Bishop Brauer-Rieke argued persuasively for this new, out-of-the-box experiment. In a way, they were standing up for the reformation of the church in the same way as their namesake, Martin Luther, had stood before papal authorities, saying, "Here I stand, I can do no other." In this instance, both sides of the argument were in the tradition of a continually reforming church, and the project was approved. The practices learned from the experience with organizing proved their worth in building the case for Leaven / Salt and Light: relational work; strong, clear proposals; steadiness in the face of tension; and moving to a negotiated agreement.

SABBATICAL

My second sabbatical made space for Leaven to gestate and develop apart from my watchful attention. It also gave me a chance to breathe the new air of my next phase of life and ministry. I worked diligently to develop a regional approach to institutional development through my IAF project, Transformational Leadership. Already beginning in 2011, I had developed a series of two-day workshops for regional leaders from religious, labor, educational, and community-based organizations. These workshops and the multiplatform relationships they facilitated inspired me. This was closer to the vision of community that Jesus proclaimed. More importantly, the power of a single sector—labor with its political savvy and religion with its strong value base, for example—could not stand alone against the tidal wave of economic power set loose by deregulation from the 1980s forward. Once in the same room, leaders from many sectors began to appreciate and agitate one another to bring about new creativity and concrete partnerships.

During one session in Seattle, I sat with a bishop, a church staff member, and a pastoral colleague in a small breakout room with one leader from Service Employees International Union (SEIU) and another from the United Association of Plumbers and Steamfitters (UA). While we found much in common in the challenges presented by shrinking memberships and the struggle to hold space in the civil sector, we also realized that labor and religion needed each other and brought different gifts. The religious leaders lamented the decline of the church and its shrinking resources, with the bishop concluding that he didn't want to preside over the closure of half the congregations under his charge. At this point, the young labor leader from SEIU, not raised a Christian but aware through his connections with religious leaders in the alliance, turned to the bishop and said, "I thought you guys believed in the resurrection." A pin dropped silently in heaven. This exchange demonstrated clearly how the mix of institutional leaders from different segments of the civil sector could build relationships, agitate, and bring new insights and energy. I hoped to continue this regional, intersectional work, but due to funding limits and the difficulty of keeping relationships throughout such a large geographic area, I had to refocus on congregations in Oregon in the next phase of Transformational Leadership in the following years. My sabbatical offered me time and space to make this transition and, frankly, to find rest and renewal for myself in the midst of an intense and complex process at Redeemer.

My sabbatical also offered me a retreat at Ring Lake Ranch with Belden Lane, author of *Backpacking with the Saints*. I also attended a family reunion in Minnesota, visited my ancestral home in Bemidji, and went to the cemetery at Ardahl Lutheran, where my grandparents and great-grandparents were buried. During this sabbatical, I also established a "table of four" with three leaders from Redeemer: Dick Harmon, Nancy Phelps, and David Damcke. I appreciate these friends as we continue to meet every month for breakfast to this day.

REDEEMER MUST DECREASE, LEAVEN MUST INCREASE

Existing Redeemer leaders and new emerging Leaven leaders stepped into new roles and assumed responsibilities for rooting the new structures and protocols in a relational organizing spiritual culture. Longtime member and leader Lois Jordahl stepped up big time in her role as Redeemer president for three consecutive terms during the process. Lois is a lifelong member of Redeemer from age two, a strong core-team leader from the POP days forward, and a trained organizer. She embodied with grace and steadiness the necessary transition work from the Redeemer side. She continues currently as a grateful member of Leaven / Salt and Light. I recall with an inner grin her comment about me in one of her annual reports: "I think we should

> "I think we should nickname Pastor Moe 'Moses' for leading us to the promised land but not enjoying it with us."

nickname Pastor Moe 'Moses' for leading us to the promised land but not enjoying it with us."

THE FINAL LAP

In January 2013, I returned from my sabbatical to behold a wonderful transformation in full bloom. The three-part plan was culminating in the final chapter for me and the new beginning for Leaven / Salt and Light in less than six months. I concluded my last annual report with some intentions:

> Looking ahead to 2013, I have two main intentions:
>
> 1. To do everything in my power to support and continue the development of the new Leaven community, and specifically to invite the elder community to an additional level of financial support through a planned giving initiative.
> 2. To prayerfully and straightforwardly say goodbye to the beloved community known as "Redeemer" collectively and individually. As with any grief process, I expect this not to be easy, nor fulfilled in the less than six months before us, though I expect a gigantic PARTY in late June to give thanks and celebrate!
>
> The sabbatical offered time to really appreciate the years at Redeemer, the people I have known and loved, many of whom are gone, and to feel the trust I have that the seed of Redeemer is growing into a new beautiful and strong community of faith.[7]

In the body of my report, I reflected deeply on my roles as pastor, leader, and organizer over three decades of ministry. I had grown so

---

[7] *Redeemer Lutheran Church Annual Report,* January 2013.

fond of the people and community of Redeemer. Now it was time to let go.

The final period of Leaven's development for me was a blend of leave taking, assisting in the development of Leaven as I could, and transitioning to a new call in organizing Transformational Leadership. The grief I was experiencing was mitigated by the tremendous joy and pride I was feeling as Leaven began to soar and about increasing clarity about my own next phase in organizing. It was my Mount Nebo. I looked out on a promised land I would not enter but would celebrate nonetheless.

A SERVICE OF REMEMBRANCE, RELEASE, AND GRATITUDE

The congregation planned a farewell service for me on June 2, 2013. That morning, I made a proposal to the accompanist and the choir that I sing a solo as part of the service. I can carry a tune, but I'm not a singer, so when I hid the microphone behind my robe and stepped into the back row of the choir, the congregation must have been surprised. As the choir swayed and hummed, I sang my soul's parting love:

> Thank you, Lord. Thank you, Lord. Thank you, Lord.
> I just want to thank you, Lord.
> Been so good. Been so good. Been so good.
> I just want to thank you, Lord.

As I looked out on the Redeemer congregation sprinkled with new Leaven folks, an ocean of faces flashed before me. Those from the congregation I had buried outnumbered the congregation that remained. A vision of the communion of saints in the heavenly realm opened in my heart. I zoomed in on glints of people I had touched and who had touched me over the last three decades. I remembered Joan Lepley, the courageous, outrageous woman who entered seminary before a door to ordination had been opened. She raised her grandchildren and suffered a paralyzing stroke that left her wordless yet even more contemplative. She went into the gracious arms of Jesus just months before Leaven, a dream she carried in her heart long before anyone else articulated it. The bush was burning and not consumed as the developing, organizing, spiritual ministry that filled my years of ministry flared before me. At the same time, I felt the potential of the new Leaven community being birthed out of long labor. We sang a new verse of "Holy, Holy, Holy" I had written for the celebration of the Eucharist. Ali Ippolito put it to music:

> Holy, Holy, Holy One. You are worthy of praise!
> Holy, Holy, Holy One, to you our heart's soul we raise!
> Amen. Blessing! Amen. Glory! Amen. Wisdom! Amen. Might!
> Amen. Thanksgiving and peace! Amen. Power and light!

My retirement party at the Sons of Norway Hall in Portland was celebrated later on with food, a live band, gratitudes from several speakers, laughter, and tears. Leaders would skate into the future without me. I was at peace. I had negotiated a call from the Oregon Synod to a special service as an organizer for IAF Northwest to develop a new initiative, Transformational Leadership, teaching and applying lessons from our Redeemer/Leaven journey and sharing wisdom from the spiritual, organizing, and organizational change sources.

The next big event on the transition timeline was the founding assembly. Before this could take place, however, the issues of membership in Leaven / Salt and Light needed to be clarified and ratified by the community. Part of the complexity of Leaven was the membership. In a congregation, the basic requirements for membership are confession of faith and baptism, attendance in worship (in the ELCA, receiving communion at least once in a given year), and financial commitment (in the ELCA, giving of record at least once in a given year). What would membership in a community-based nonprofit dedicated to exploring spirituality and organizing for justice look like? Here's what leaders discerned and presented at Leaven's founding assembly:

MEMBER COVENANT

This is the covenant for Leaven and Salt and Light Lutheran Church. Membership cards can be completed online or in person at our community center. Those committed to Salt and Light and Leaven seek to live out this membership in spirit and practice to the best of our ability within the confines of our current legal structure.

A Voting Member of Leaven

- publicly and/or formally commits to membership and the vision of Leaven
- honors the experience, creativity, and imagination of all generations, genders, ethnic and cultural groups, and the broad fabric of our community
- makes individual connections by telling their story to another person and listening to the story of another person
- participates authentically in activities that nurture connection with humanity, cosmos, and spirit
- attends a minimum of three Leaven activities per year
- commits to support the vision of Leaven by making a contribution of record at least once per calendar year to Leaven

A Salt and Light Voting Member*

- has been baptized
- has been confirmed and/or publicly commits to a journey of faith in this congregation and community
- shares in Holy Communion at least once a year

*All voting members of Salt and Light congregation are automatically members of Leaven, thus all the Leaven commitments apply also to Salt and Light members. The congregational expectations are in addition to Leaven's.

Membership of Children

We value the presence, creativity, and voices of the children, and their participation is welcomed as a vital part of our community at all gatherings and in our life together. In conversation with parents and organizational leadership, a child may become a voting member of Leaven and/or Salt and Light when she/he reaches an appropriate age and has developed an interest in more formal decision-making participation.

Anyone, regardless of membership, is warmly invited to partner with Leaven and Salt and Light Lutheran Church as they are moved and have interest. Leaven is BIGGER than our membership.

FOUNDING A NEW LEAVEN COMMUNITY

The founding assembly followed the pattern of IAF organizations. During the three or more years of incubation funded by sponsors—in Leaven's case, the property sale and other funding sources—organizers could work freely without worrying (too much) about funding. Now it was time for Leaven to walk on its own. Leaven's founding assembly was envisioned at the beginning of the eighteen-month plan but came into focus in the final six months. Its design included the following:

- roll call and recognition of members and leaders
- relational meetings
- stories
- history of Redeemer ("Little Redeemer Riding Hood Meets the Three Bears")
- recognition of accomplishments leading up to the assembly

- spiritual grounding (sermon by Pastor Reed)
- call to action: commitments to membership in the new entities, Leaven and Salt and Light (note: all members of Salt and Light were automatically members of Leaven, but Leaven members could be members without joining the Lutheran congregation)

"LITTLE REDEEMER RIDING HOOD MEETS THE THREE BEARS"

A history of Redeemer could have been really boring, a killer. The creative Damaris Webb, daughter of elders Ben and Vi Webb and an outstanding actor, playwright, and producer, made sure the "history" was anything but boring! She invited us to produce a play using a genre of our choice. We chose the genre of fairy tale and called it "Little Redeemer Riding Hood Meets the Three Bears." It was a hoot. Here's an excerpt:

> Little Redeemer Riding Hood (LRRH) is going through a dark wood looking for Gramma's Church. Of course, she doesn't find it. At one point, she falls to the ground in exasperation:
>
> **LRRH:** Yes, I tried to do lots of stuff. Some things were too soft, and some things too hard. Some were too cold, and some were too hot. I wanted to buy a beautiful ebony piano because it would make happy music. But part of me wondered if we should spend the money, and part of me doesn't like change, even if it's for the better. I was all mixed up inside. All my voices were going in all different directions. And I was all emotional. Things were changing in my core!
>
> Later she reflects on a vision beginning to emerge:
>
> **LRRH:** What if we built a larger, more mixed and spiritual community right here in the woods? And all the forest

creatures could gather when the wolves howl, both inside and out, and we could learn how to work together to create a healthy forest?

Finally, she recognizes the transformation that had been years in the making. She is dizzy and giddy. She falls to the ground.

> **LRRH:** Oh, I'm feeling faint. My head is swirling. What was in that potion you gave me? What happened?
> Other voices:
> You're alright! You've just changed!
> You are now Salt and Light.
> Yes, you are a little leaven for the whole loaf.[8]

The headline in the Leaven news after the founding assembly read, "We Are Leaven. We Are Salt and Light! Whew! Let's Eat, Everyone."

Wendy Hall Curtis went on to summarize the day:

- We founded a new nonprofit organization called Leaven. It's an emerging community that focuses on exploring spirituality and organizing for justice.
- We founded a Lutheran congregation that is part of Leaven, called Salt and Light Lutheran Church. It's what's known as a "mission congregation."
- We honored Redeemer Lutheran Church and gave thanks as she became Salt and Light.
- We gave thanks and honored Pastor Terry Moe, who was the pastor of Redeemer Lutheran for over thirty-two years and is moving into a new role as pastor/organizer with a new organization.[9]

---

[8] From *Little Redeemer Riding Hood Meets the Three Bears*, a brief play written mostly by me with input from many and directed and produced by Damaris Webb.
[9] *Leaven News*, July 2013.

THE SIGNIFICANCE OF "THREE AND A HALF"

I have come to appreciate the symbolism of numbers found in certain apocalyptic books. I discovered that three and a half, the time in years of Redeemer's transition to Leaven / Salt and Light, is a number associated with halfway to the holy number of seven. In Daniel, for example, three and a half is expressed as "one thousand two hundred ninety days" or more (I'm not sure of the math, though both are close to three and a half years): "From the time that the regular burnt offering is taken away and the abomination that desolates is set up, there shall be one thousand two hundred ninety days. Happy are those who persevere and attain the thousand three hundred and thirty-five days."[10]

Similarly, in Revelation, three and a half is expressed as "Similarly, in Revelation, three and a half is expressed as 'forty-two months' in one place, and 'one thousand two hundred sixty days' in the next verse."[11]

Three and a half is the midpoint on the way to the perfect number seven. Leaven hasn't reached perfection. It is still unfolding, but after one thousand two hundred and sixty days of spirituality and organizing, it has grown into a thriving, postmodern faith community.

BLESSING

I found a blessing to share with Redeemer-becoming-Leaven from Mary McLeod Bethune's "Last Will and Testament." This Black educator (1875–1955) was a civil rights pioneer and an important mentor for Rev. Howard Thurman and other Black leaders. The items she "wills" are appropriate as a blessing for the church:

I leave you love.
I leave you hope.

10 Daniel 12:11–12 NRSV.
11 Revelation 11:2–3 NRSV.

I leave you the challenge of developing confidence in one
    another.
I leave you a thirst for education.
I leave you responsibility for the use of power.
I leave you faith.
I leave you racial dignity.
I leave you a desire to live harmoniously with your fellow
    man.
I leave you a responsibility to our young people.[12]

It was a fitting ending for the founding of Leaven and for my adventure serving Redeemer (which was also very close to three and a half decades). Redeemer died. Leaven rose. The transformation continues. The bush still burns (https://www.leaven.org). "Lord God, you have called your servants to ventures of which we cannot see the ending, by paths as yet untrodden, through perils unknown. Give us faith to go out with good courage, not knowing where we go, but only that your hand is leading us and your love supporting us; through Jesus Christ our Lord. Amen."[13]

> Redeemer died. Leaven rose. The transformation continues. The bush still burns.

FOR REFLECTION

Pastor Reed and Pastor Moe, with outside help, had developed a good transition plan. Chapter 11 is the final lap for Redeemer and Pastor Moe. It is the starting gate for Pastor Reed and the new community, Leaven / Salt and Light.

---

[12] Excerpted from Laurent A. Parks, Cheryl H. Keen, James B. Keen, and Sharon Daloz Parks, *Common Fire: Leadership Lives of Commitment in a Complex World* (Boston: Beacon, 1997), 81.

[13] *Lutheran Book of Worship*, 153.

- What rituals, actions, and decisions help us say good-bye and hello?
- What rituals, actions, and decisions are you making as you face endings and new beginnings?

For Pastor Moe, the time of sabbatical and conscientious planning of a good closure eased the pain of leaving a beloved community after more than thirty-two years.

- How have you strategically planned for your own transitions in life and profession?
- How equipped is your congregation for these transitions?
- How are you building a capacity for inevitable change, even transformation? For yourself? For your organization?

12 THE BUSH STILL BURNS

And God said further to Moses, "Thus you shall speak to the Isra-elites: The Lord, the God of your fathers, the God of Abraham, the God of Isaac, and the God of Jacob, has sent me to you: This shall be My name forever, This My appellation for all eternity."[1]

—Exodus 3:15

The "burning bush" is not a miracle. It was a test. God wanted to find out whether or not Moses could pay attention to something for more than a few minutes. When Moses did, God Spoke.[2]

—Lawrence Kushner

In Kierkegaard's most famous words: "Life must be lived forward, but it can be understood only backwards." And as Mark Twain put it in his inimitable style, "Although the past may not repeat itself, it does rhyme."[3]

—*The Spirituality of Imperfection*

SPIRITUALITY AND ORGANIZING ARE COMBINING IN AMAZING WAYS IN congregations and judicatories across the country. The playing field is growing. Courageous and innovative spiritually based organizing leaders are rising up. Congregations are breaking open and making dramatic shifts as pressures make them focus on imagining and creating alternative futures.

---

[1] Exodus 3:15, JPS H-ET.
[2] Lawrence Kushner, *God Was in This Place and I, I Did Not Know It* (Woodstock, VA: Jewish Lights, 1991), 25.
[3] Kurtz and Ketcham, *The Spirituality of Imperfection*, 153.

The Bush Still Burns is one story of how the Spirit worked miracles in a traditional congregation among ordinary people, bringing transformation to individuals, the congregation, and the community. I offer this story not as a recipe for success but as an example of how the Spirit used our attempts at opening ourselves spiritually and guided our engagement with organizing to bring about transformation. May this story inspire others to apply spirituality and organizing to their congregation in new and transformational ways.

Redeemer and I started from the ground up. We hadn't heard of community organizing. We weren't aware of spirituality other than the hymnal we used in Sunday worship. We shied away from deeper spirituality. Organizing and spirituality were both foreign languages we had to learn. We had to rebuild the house while we were living in it. At the same time, we were learning the skills of building—what tools to use, what went where, and in what order things needed to be put together. Redeemer was learning and applying the heart shifts that the wells of spirituality brought and integrating the arts, skills, and mindset of organizing in an existing congregation. We did this building from the ground up without a blueprint. And while we started to build something new, we needed to pay attention to the regular responsibilities of congregational life. Of course, we made mistakes. It took a long time.

Does it have to take so long? Do congregations have enough time?

Pastor Reed had the advantage of learning both spirituality and organizing in her twenties. She came much more ready to take things to a higher level. Maximizing the gifts of contemplative organizing for the church and the world requires a major shift in thinking and a new set of practices. This shift is happening sporadically now in some places, but it can be accelerated through strategic interventions. Denominations, seminaries, local judicatories, congregations, and individual leaders inside and outside the church need to participate. Others are starting at a place already down the road from where Redeemer started.

For example, Rev. Erika Spaet, a recent graduate of PLTS, is developing Story-Dwelling, a new faith community in Bend, Oregon, as a joint Lutheran-Methodist effort. Erika discerned her call to ministry at Redeemer-becoming-Leaven, where she engaged and deepened her calling to contemplative organizing. Rev. Solveig Nilsen-Goodin, an early intern at Redeemer, applied spirituality and organizing in her work as a mission developer for Wilderness Way, an innovative and justice-oriented faith community. Rev. Robyn Hartwig, also an early intern at Redeemer, has developed a national network, Eco-Faith Recovery, built on the leadership development practices of organizing and the spirituality of church and twelve-step recovery. Bonnie Beadles-Bohling, a lay leader from Central Lutheran, Portland, reengaged her childhood calling to ministry through Transformational Leadership. She was consecrated in 2019 as a deacon in the Lutheran Church and called to contemplative organizing. These are just a few of many who have already been impacted by turning to the burning bush of prayer and organizing. Imagine who else is already engaged. More importantly, imagine who could be engaged, developed, and transformed with intentional turning to the bush all aflame!

A MASSIVE SHIFT FROM SERVICE/ADVOCACY TO ORGANIZING?

National church bodies can shift resources from service and advocacy to organizing in order to address the upstream causes of local problems. Saul Alinsky was critical of social service primarily because he thought it disempowered the poor. John McKnight argues powerfully in a similar vein in an article, "Why 'Servanthood' Is Bad," written in 1989.[4] Instead, the church could embrace what Bonhoeffer called the view from below, joining church and world in a common struggle for equity and justice that the God of Moses and Jesus desires. Martin Luther King Jr. preaches the good news of the Good Samaritan with

---

[4] John McKnight, "Why Servanthood Is Bad," *Other Side*, January/February 1989, 30.

a twist: "On the one hand we are called to play the good Samaritan on life's roadside; but that will only be an initial act. One day we must come to see that the whole Jericho road must be transformed so that men and women will not be constantly beaten and robbed as they make their journey on life's highway. True compassion is more than flinging a coin to a beggar; it is not haphazard and superficial. It comes to see that an edifice which produces beggars needs restructuring."[5]

Rev. Susan Engh, former director for congregation-based organizing in the ELCA, organized with Pastor Melissa Reed and other leaders to form the Organizing for Mission Cohort, a national community of practice for leaders seeking to integrate organizing and spirituality into new and existing ministries. This has become a seedbed for new energy and capacity for the church and the world. Rev. Engh's recent book, *Women's Work: The Transformational Power of Faith-Based Community Organizing,* tells the story of women leaders and pastors making a difference in communities across the country. It includes relevant sections about Rev. Melissa Reed. How will the church today respond to the many Jericho roads? It is time to organize with true compassion.

Seminaries play a vital role. The teaching of the arts, practices, mindset, and relational culture of power needs to be instilled early on in the formation of both lay and clergy leaders. Under the leadership of Rev. Dr. Ray Pickett, PLTS is leading the way in grounding lay and clergy leadership in organizing and spirituality both academically and practically. PLTS called Dr. Pickett with eyes wide open to the radical vision he shared. Now students are grounded in contemplative organizing at the core of a curriculum and practicum oriented to form transformational lay and clergy leaders. PLTS works in collaboration with ten synods.

Synods and judicatory bodies can also play a key role by investing in leadership grounded in spirituality and organizing for the

---

[5] Martin Luther King Jr. sermon, "A Time to Break Silence," at Riverside Church, April 4, 1967.

sake of shifting the cultures of congregations that are floundering and therefore open to something new. Redeemer was able to grow a fund of nearly a million dollars to invest in developing Leaven / Salt and Light alongside Redeemer. What might denominational entities be able to raise and invest strategically in new experiments based on organizing and spirituality? How might regional bodies invest in lay and professional leadership? Church judicatories could lead the way for congregations to participate in local organizing affiliates and transformational communities of practice throughout regions.

In Oregon, for example, Dave Brauer-Rieke, bishop of the Oregon Synod, 2007–19, used the IAF weeklong training and Transformational Leadership to shift the culture of the synod. Newly elected bishop Laurie Larson-Caesar, installed on December 15, 2019, is breaking new ground in connecting church and world. Pastor Melissa Reed, who developed Leaven, is now bishop's associate for vital leadership and sacramental organizing. Colleague Juan Carlos la Puente Tapia also brings the gifts of spirituality and organizing to his work as bishop's associate for intercultural and interreligious mission.

The church needs to partner more closely with organizing entities grounded in sound practices and strategies. The church alone cannot organize effectively given the massive power of the market sector. IAF and other organizing efforts bring together organizations of labor, education, and community-based nonprofits in an organization of organizations that can garner enough power to stand its ground against the postmodern swell of pyramids and storehouses. This is a contentious, critical, and challenging discernment. Will the church remain in its silo or join others of goodwill in the work of God in the world?

> Will the church remain in its silo or join others of goodwill in the work of God in the world?

One of the shortcomings of organizing entities is their focus on big-city arenas. Certainly, that's where much of the action is. However, in Oregon and other parts of the country, many congregations live and move and have their being outside metropolitan areas. These town and country congregations also need their voices to be heard at the tables of power. Upon leaving Redeemer when Leaven was founded, I initiated a project called Transformational Leadership that built local cohorts in suburban, rural, and midsized towns in Oregon. Local part-time leader/organizers, both lay and clergy, invited congregations, schools, and community groups to organize in communities of practice (COPs) to bring the gifts of spirit-based organizing to more parts of Oregon. While this project did not build long-lasting COPs, it is an experiment worth pursuing.

CHURCH AND WORLD AT THE SAME TIME

The church cannot remain isolated in its religious silo as if God were only active in that part of the world. Broad-based organizing brings the opportunity to discover the gifts of the other. Scripture illustrates how those considered outsiders bring God's blessings and act in "godly" ways. Think of Jethro, the priest of Midian, Ruth the Moabite, Cyrus the Persian, and the unknown healer casting out demons in Mark 9, to name a few: "John said to him, 'Teacher, we saw someone casting out demons in your name, and we tried to stop him, because he was not following us.' But Jesus said, 'Do not stop him; for no one who does a deed of power in my name will be able soon afterwards to speak evil of me. Whoever is not against us is for us. For truly I tell you, whoever gives you a cup of water to drink because you bear the name of Christ will by no means lose the reward.' "[6]

Furthermore, many folks in the community are hungry for the wells of deep spirituality coupled with effective organizing to make the world better. Some will come to a deeper spirituality through action. Others move out based on their spiritual awakening. I am convinced that many people are allergic to a church, synagogue, or other religious organizations that lack this connection.

[6] Mark 9:38–41 NRSV.

People want to be part of an effective action-oriented organization rooted in faith values. Where will they find vehicles for training, action, reflection, and prayer if not in congregations and the networks that support them? Dietrich Bonhoeffer keenly combines a God-and-the-world-at-the-same-time approach. It is a key theological premise undergirding a mix of churchly and worldly organizing that invites the church into God and the world at the same time:

> In Christ we are invited to participate in the reality of God and the reality of the world at the same time, the one not without the other. The reality of God is disclosed only as it places me completely into the reality of the world. But I find the reality of the world always already borne, accepted, and reconciled in the reality of God. That is the mystery of the revelation of God in the human being Jesus Christ. . . . What matters is participating in the reality of God and the world in Jesus Christ today, and in doing so in such a way that I never experience the reality of God without the reality of the world, nor the reality of the world without the reality of God.[7]

Finally, it is time to recognize that the church exists in a changed and increasingly distracting, alluring, and even hostile culture. The church grew dramatically following World War II, and in that culture, most of our existing congregations thrived. But recent decades have brought dramatic shifts. Like a frog in water that is gradually heated up, the church is being seduced into a sleepiness unto death.[8]

More importantly, the church and the world are in the same pot. As the heat is turned up socially, economically, and ecologically, both the church and the world are threatened. The earth is a frog in a pot of warming water. The church must find a role as the world heats up, and churches must be open to views outside

---

[7] Dietrich Bonhoeffer, *Ethics, Dietrich Bonhoeffer Works, English Edition*, vol. 6 (Minneapolis: Fortress, 2005), 55.
[8] Peter Senge, *The Fifth Discipline: The Art and Practice of the Learning Organization* (New York: Doubleday), 22–23.

their world. Otto Scharmer and Katrina Kaufer[9] bring a clear, comprehensive, and challenging analysis to the table, an analysis the church should take seriously. Their premise is that we face three great divides: ecological, spiritual-cultural, and socioeconomic. We are disconnected from these realities and therefore end up organizing for results that nobody really wants. Often, these metalevel realities are complex, intertwined, and persistent chasms, which congregations must face in microframeworks, as we at Redeemer discovered in our organizing work.

As I read and studied Scharmer's works, I became more and more intrigued. I staggered as I read, "Think of our attention and our ability to pay attention as the sacred space that we want to savor, protect, and cultivate because it is our well of strength and well-being. We know how much attention matters. . . . So what is the current state of our sacred space? Under attack!"[10]

I thought seriously about attending a weeklong seminar offered by Scharmer's Presencing Institute. I wanted to learn and to share my perspective as a faith leader, feeling that this perspective was indeed present but thin in their experience. Then I discovered the $10,000 cost of the seminar and backed off. Still, it is the kind of table the church must engage.

The 2018 book *A Finer Future: Creating an Economy in Service to Life* delves more deeply into the socioeconomic divides of our country. It reiterates and builds upon research on the impacts of massive economic shifts in the decades after World War II,[11] shifts that unfolded under our watch as the water in our pot warmed. It confirms what many of us intuited, that the rich were getting richer and the poor getting poorer: from 1947 to 1979, we all grew together economically. It was a period in which most boats were rising; from 1979 to 2014, we grew apart. For example, in the postwar

---

[9] See Otto C. Scharmer and Katrin Kaufer, *Leading from the Emerging Future: From Ego-System to Eco-System Economies* (San Francisco: Berrett-Koehler, 2013).

[10] Scharmer and Kaufer, *Leading from the Emerging Future*, 106.

[11] Hunter Lovins, Stewart Wallis, Anders Wijkman, and John Fullerton, *A Finer Future: Creating an Economy in Service to Life* (Gabriola Island, BC, Canada: New Society, 2018), 36.

period, the bottom 20 percent of the population grew economically by 116 percent, a healthy growth for a thirty-year period. At the same time, the top 1 percent grew by 61 percent. Much of this uniform growth was the result of policies of the New Deal after the Great Depression that regulated banks and utilities and prevented huge monopolies. In the post-1979 period, however, the bottom 20 percent actually diminished by 12 percent, while the top 1 percent grew by a whopping 162 percent. This was a clear picture of what was shifting in the period when Redeemer began to organize. The pressures on our households in all congregations across the country traced their source back to this primary economic shift.

LESSONS LEARNED AND BEING LEARNED

Along the way, I learned valuable lessons. Here are just some:

- Don't do it alone (teams of all kinds—core team, interim teams)!
- Diagnose the system before acting (e.g., red-piano incident, Central City 2000 Task Force).
- Focus on power over program (money in hand or committed, strong relational leadership).
- Make sure to focus on relationships—even when they are difficult (one-to-ones, small groups, assemblies, lots of leaders)!
- Include the center and the edges (dealing with status quo requires lots of attention to the old and new).
- Know that it takes time (it can't be rushed, but you can't let it unwind either).

THE MYSTERY OF THE ACTION OF GOD

As I step back from my more-than-thirty-year odyssey, I am aware of how deeply and graciously the Spirit has led me. I often was unaware of that leading, but at times, I saw with eyes wide open. For many years, I have searched for language to carry the message of what Jesus called the kingdom of God. *Kingdom* is a key concept in Jesus's ministry, but it can get mixed up with images of place, castles, dungeons, patriarchy, and the abusive use of power. Many words have been suggested as substitutes for *kingdom*. Each is somewhat helpful but not quite on the mark: *realm, reign, household, economy, empire of the heavens*, and so on. One day I woke up in the middle of the night with a phrase in my head: "The Mystery of the Action of God." It isn't the answer, but for me, it combines the spiritual and organizing dimensions of God's "kingdom."

> The mystery moves like the wind, blowing when and where it will.

The purpose of action is to get a reaction. God acts. Humans react. The mystery moves like the wind, blowing when and where it will. Applying this metaphor to familiar parables helps me see how the Spirit is acting in order to get our attention and reaction:

> The mystery of the action of God is like a treasure in a field that someone discovers. The discoverer goes out and sells all that they have in order to buy that field.
>
> The mystery of the action of God is like a merchant in search of fine pearls who, when they find a pearl of great value, goes and sells all they have in order to buy that pearl.
>
> The mystery of the action of God is like a little yeast that a woman folds into her dough to make it rise.

The mystery of the action of God is like a congregation that turns to the burning bush in contemplative organizing and is transformed into a whole new entity. May you see, turn toward, and listen to the bush all aflame today.

DAYENU

Dayenu[12] is sung as part of the Jewish Passover holiday. The song is about being grateful to God for all the gifts God gave the Jewish people, such as taking them out of slavery, giving them the Torah and Shabbat, and more. Fifteen stanzas represent fifteen gifts given during the Exodus. The word *dayenu* means "it would have been enough," "it would have been sufficient," "it would have sufficed." It is the faith of the Hebrews that if all had not been accomplished as it was, it would have been enough.

For example,

> If God had brought us out of Egypt but not carried out
> judgments against them—
> Dayenu! It would have sufficed!
> If God had split the sea for us but not taken us through it on
> dry land—
> Dayenu! It would have sufficed!

One of the longtime members of Redeemer once said, "You know, if this hadn't worked, if we had run out of money, or people hadn't stepped up, or leaders left in discouragement, it still would have been worth it because seeds have been planted." *Dayenu!*

> If God had planted seeds of spirituality and organizing in the
> bones of Redeemer but no new vision had arisen—*Dayenu! It
> would have sufficed!*
> If Redeemer had prayed and organized and not created
> affordable housing or mitigated the effects of a large-scale sewer
> project—*Dayenu! It would have sufficed!*
> If Redeemer had not struggled to discover a red piano in
> the midst of a chasm—*Dayenu! It would have sufficed!*

---

12 https://en.wikipedia.org/wiki/Dayenu.

If the congregation had not died to become a nurse log for the future—*Dayenu! It would have sufficed!*

If all the interns had not contributed their slice of new hope and vision—*Dayenu! It would have sufficed!*

If the opportunity to sell property and raise enough money to pay three salaries had not been organized and implemented—*Dayenu! It would have sufficed!*

If God had brought new visions but Redeemer had failed to plan for new life—*Dayenu! It would have sufficed!*

If God had not sent the beloved saints and leaders by paths as yet untrodden through perils unknown—*Dayenu! It would have sufficed!*

If Intern Melissa Reed had not become Outreach Pastor Melissa Reed, and then Mission Developer Organizer Melissa Reed, and then Leaven Codirector/Pastor Melissa Reed—*Dayenu! It would have sufficed!*

In small measure, compared to the Exodus miracles, I'm so glad God did all these things, even if without them, it would have been enough.

FOR REFLECTION

This chapter summarizes the role of spirituality and organizing in a Spirit-led transformation of pastor and people. It's not the only way—it's a way.

- What value do you see in organizing and spirituality for your congregation?
- How do the components of organizing and spirituality fit your organization in its current form? How could it fit going forward?

Chapter 12 boldly asserts that faith communities need to shift from service/advocacy to organizing. Many want to do both, something Pastor Moe believes is neither desirable nor helpful for a variety of reasons.

- How do you respond to the challenge of moving from service to organizing?
- If you want to shift, what are the strategies, practices, and support needed?

The conclusion is a challenge to multilevel engagement from the individual leader to the local institution to the larger entities surrounding the local institutions such as national and regional bodies, seminaries, and educational institutions.

- How do you see your engagement with other partner organizations?
- How have you seen these also struggle to shift and change?

EPILOGUE

IT IS AUDACIOUS TO INVOKE PARALLELS BETWEEN MOSES'S STORY AND ANY small, local story like Redeemer's.[1] At the same time, many similarities exist and invite you to reflect on your own experiences of having a call and following it. Here are some of the similarities drawn in this book:

- Moses was born Hebrew and raised Egyptian. Redeemer was founded as a working-class congregation that began to see how it had been seduced into a worldview in conflict with its best values and aspirations. In short, the congregation discovered it wasn't in Kansas anymore.
- Moses ran away from Egypt and hid out as a shepherd (pastor) in Midian. The pastor and people of Redeemer tried to hide out in the corner of Northeast Twentieth and Killingsworth as a traditional Lutheran congregation still living as we had in the 1950s.
- Moses awakened to a vision of a bush all aflame. Redeemer, through spirituality and organizing, began to wake up to a burning bush.
- Moses turned aside and paid attention to the bush. Why was it not consumed? Redeemer pondered its new circumstances in prayer, action, and reflection. Why didn't Redeemer go away?
- Moses and Redeemer both wrestled with the angel/Spirit/God, who began to speak when they turned aside to pay attention. Both had questions to probe and inadequacies to be addressed. Moses

---

[1] See the website www.stillburningbush.org for more on Moses, transformation, spirituality, and organizing.

seems to stride back to Egypt. Redeemer moved gingerly toward embracing a spirituality and organizing mode very different from its past. It took a long while to face the brave new world of the thirty-year period from 1981 to 2013 covered in the book.

• Scholars aren't clear if a lag existed between Moses's encounter with the bush all aflame and his return to Egypt. Tradition says that Moses's life can be divided into neat forty-year periods: forty in Egypt, forty in Midian, forty in the wilderness. When the bush all aflame appeared, one would assume he needed some time to assimilate, prepare, and then move on. The story in the Book of Exodus, however, makes no mention of training, preparation, and further integration of the calling. Chapters 3 and 4 are in Midian. By chapter 5, Moses and Aaron are back in Egypt. Redeemer's story is a long awakening. Awareness of growing economic disparity, racism, addiction, incarceration, war, new pressures on families, and many other things led Redeemer to a long discernment to move toward liberation.

• In the end, Moses and Redeemer used both sides of their identity to move forward. Moses, having been raised Egyptian, knew the ins and outs of Pharaoh's court. His skill and insight as an Egyptian were invaluable in the confrontations to come. Still, he was Hebrew at heart. Redeemer claimed its privilege and power in the world as it is, though it had to learn the ever-shifting ways of government and business. This began to blend with Redeemer's own immigrant roots and predominantly working-class identity. Both were invaluable in the organizing, spirituality, and transformation God precipitated.

In both stories, the flaming bush appeared, and leaders turned aside to pay attention. Only then did a voice come. After objecting, arguing, wondering, questioning, procrastinating, ruminating, and praying, both engaged the hegemony of Egypt using their Hebrew and Egyptian sides. Near the end of the story in Exodus 3, God reveals a new identity: "I am who I am" or "I will be who I will be" or "I am becoming who I am becoming." These are all familiar to most of us as readers of this story. In the course of study for this book, I discovered a new identity that, for me, makes greater sense of the story and propels the story forward to all generations, in part validating the audacious claim of identification with Moses.

Martin Buber proposes a different interpretation for the Hebrew phrase "Ehyeh-Asher-Ehyeh": "This is usually understood to mean 'I am that I am' in the sense that YHVH describes himself as the Being One or even the Everlasting One, the one unfalteringly persisting in his being."[2]

Buber's critique is that this interpretation is existential, abstract, even remote. This is like saying "Well, of course I believe in God" but not having really any life impact as a result of that belief. Buber then nails it. (Please excuse Buber's use of the male pronouns, a reflection of his time. The author decided not to change Buber's language and believes if Buber were alive today, he would have discovered new language for what he is saying.) "YHVH is 'He who will be present' or 'He who is here'; he who is present here; not merely some time and some where but in every now and every here. Now the name expresses his character and assures the faithful of the richly protective presence of their Lord."[3]

> "YHVH is 'He who will be present' or 'He who is here'; he who is present here; not merely some time and some where but in every now and every here."

The import of this is that God doesn't just exist somewhere, sometime, but that God is present, available, engaged. God has come down to dwell with us, to lead and guide us, to call, enlighten, gather, and send us. This is good news from the bush all aflame and the angel/God who speaks.

[2] Martin Buber, "The Burning Bush," in *Moses: The Revelation and the Covenant* (New York: Harper, 1958), 39–55.
[3] Buber, "Burning Bush," 53.

Moses heard and responded in a spirituality and organizing mode. Indeed, Redeemer, now Leaven / Salt and Light, recognizes and gives thanks that this Holy Present One has been, is, and will be with us and is, has been, and will be present for all who are called by holy fire.

Soli Deo Gloria
www.leaven.org
www.stillburningbush.org

SELECT BIBLIOGRAPHY

Alexander, Michelle. *The New Jim Crow: Mass Incarceration in the Age of Colorblindness.* New York: New Press, 2010.

Alinsky, Saul D. *Reveille for Radicals.* New York: Vintage, 1969.

———. *Rules for Radicals: A Pragmatic Primer for Realistic Radicals.* New York: Vintage, 1971.

Asher, Moshe ben, and Kulda bat Sarah. "Congregational Organizing: Relationship-Driven Leadership Development." *Organizing*, Spring 1995, 40–48.

Bass, Diana Butler. *Christianity after Religion: The End of Church and the Beginning of a New Spiritual Awakening.* New York: HarperCollins, 2012.

———. *Christianity for the Rest of Us: How the Neighborhood Church Is Transforming the Faith.* New York: HarperOne, 2007.

Bergan, Jacqueline Syrup, and S. Marie Schwan. *Birth: A Guide to Prayer.* Take and Receive Series. Winona, MN: St. Mary's, 1985.

Bolsinger, Tod. *Canoeing the Mountains: Christian Leadership in Uncharted Territory.* Downers Grove, IL: Intervarsity, 2015.

Bonhoeffer, Dietrich. *Ethics, Dietrich Bonhoeffer Works, English Edition.* Vol. 6. Minneapolis: Fortress, 2005.

Brewin, Kester. *Signs of Emergence: A Vision for Church That Is Organic/ Networked/Decentralized/Bottom-Up/Communal/Flexible (Always Evolving).* Grand Rapids, MI: Baker, 2007.

Brueggemann, Walter. *Hope within History.* Atlanta: John Knox, 1987.

———. *Out of Babylon.* Nashville, TN: Abingdon, 2010.

———. *The Prophetic Imagination.* Minneapolis: Fortress, 1978.

Buber, Martin. "The Burning Bush." In *Moses: The Revelation and the Covenant,* 39–55. New York: Harper, 1958.

Chambers, Edward. *Roots for Radicals: Organizing for Power, Action and Justice.* New York: Bloomsbury, 2003.

Dykstra, Craig. "A Way of Seeing: Imagination and the Pastoral Life." *Christian Century* 125, no. 7 (2008): 26–31.

Engh, Susan L. *Women's Work: The Transformational Power of Faith-Based Community Organizing.* Lanham, MD: Lexington Books / Fortress Academic, 2019.

Gecan, Michael. *Effective Organizing for Congregational Renewal.* Skokie, IL: ACTA, 2008.

———. *Going Public: An Organizer's Guide to Citizen Action.* Boston: Beacon, 2002.

Greider, William. *Who Will Tell the People? The Betrayal of American Democracy.* New York: Simon and Schuster, 1992.

Gutierrez, Gustavo. *We Drink from Our Own Wells: The Spiritual Journey of a People.* Maryknoll, NY: Orbis, 1984.

Heifetz, Ronald, Alexander Grashow, and Marty Linksy. *The Practice of Adaptive Leadership: Tools and Tactics for Changing Your Organization and the World.* Boston: Harvard Business Press, 2009.

Hughes, Patricia M. *Grace Space: Working Better Together.* Seattle: Center for Ethical Leadership, 2004.

Jacobsen, Dennis, *Doing Justice: Congregations and Community Organizing.* 2nd ed. Minneapolis: Fortress, 2017.

Kurtz, Ernest, and Katherine Ketcham. *The Spirituality of Imperfection: Storytelling and the Search for Meaning.* New York: Bantam, 1992.

Lovins, L. Hunter, Stewart Wallis, Anders Wijkman, and John Fullerton. *A Finer Future: Creating an Economy in Service to Life.* Gabriola Island, BC, Canada: New Society, 2018.

McKenzie, John L. "Moses." In *Dictionary of the Bible*, 586–90. Milwaukee: Bruce, 1965.

McKnight, John. "Why 'Servanthood' Is Bad." *Other Side*, January/February 1989, 38–41.

Moe, Terry Allen. "O Healing River: Just Prayer and Organizing." DMin thesis, Wesley Theological Seminary, 1998.

Neumark, Heidi. *Breathing Space: A Spiritual Journey in the South Bronx.* Boston: Beacon, 2003.

———. *Hidden Inheritance: Family Secrets, Memory and Faith.* Nashville, TN: Abingdon, 2015.

Niebuhr, Reinhold. *Leaves from the Notebook of a Tamed Cynic.* Louisville, KY: Westminster / John Knox, 1990.

Parks, Sharon Daloz. *Leadership Can Be Taught.* Boston: Harvard Business Press, 2005.

Pierce, Gregory F. Augustine. *Activism That Makes Sense: Congregations and Community Organization*. Chicago: ACTA, 1997.

Scharmer, Otto C. *Theory U: Leading from the Future as It Emerges*. San Francisco: Berrett-Koehler, 2009.

Scharmer, Otto, and Katrin Kaufer. *Leading from the Emerging Future: From Ego-System to Eco-System Economies*. San Francisco: Berrett-Koehler, 2013.

Schutz, Aaron, and Mike Miller, eds. *People Power: The Community Organizing Tradition of Saul Alinsky*. Nashville, TN: Vanderbilt University Press, 2015.

Senge, Peter. *The Fifth Discipline: The Art and Practice of the Learning Organization*. New York: Doubleday, 1990.

Senge, Peter, Otto C. Scharmer, Joseph Jaworski, and Betty Sue Flowers. *Presence: Human Purpose and the Field of the Future*. New York: Crown, 2004.

Singh, Kathleen Dowling. *The Grace of Dying: How We Are Transformed Spiritually as We Die*. New York: HarperCollins, 2000.

Townes, Emilie M., ed. *A Troubling in My Soul: Womanist Perspectives on Evil and Suffering*. Maryknoll, NY: Orbis, 1993.

Tutu, Desmond Mpilo. *No Future without Forgiveness*. New York: Doubleday, 1999.

Twist, Lynne. *The Soul of Money: Reclaiming the Wealth of Our Inner Resources*. New York: W. W. Norton, 2003.

Wilkerson, Isabel. *The Warmth of Other Suns: The Epic Story of America's Great Migration*. New York: Vintage, 2010.

Wink, Walter. *Engaging the Powers: Discernment and Resistance in a World of Domination*. Minneapolis: Fortress, 1992.

———. *Naming the Powers: The Language of Power in the New Testament*. Minneapolis: Fortress, 1984.

———. *Unmasking the Powers: The Invisible Forces That Determine Human Existence*. Minneapolis: Fortress, 1986.

Zornberg, Avivah Gottlieb. *Moses: A Human Life*. New Haven, CT: Yale University Press, 2016.

———. *The Particulars of Rapture: Reflections on Exodus*. New York: Schocken, 2001.

APPENDIX 1

THE RELATIONAL MEETING:
THE CORNERSTONE OF ORGANIZING

The person initiating the individual meeting—organizer, pastor, veteran leader—understands that the time devoted to individual meetings is more important than time spent in more conventional activities. "All real living," said theologian Martin Buber, "is meeting." The initiator knows that the new dynamic created by meeting and relating to another person is rich with opportunity and possibility.[4]

What a relational meeting (individual meeting, one-to-one) is *not* and what it *is*:

not a pastoral visit	*is* a mutual conversation
not an interview	*is* story based
not a sales pitch	*is* probing for passions/interests
not endless	*is* intentional and limited to 30–45 min
not information or data	*is* about building a relationship
not ideological argument	*is* about respecting the other's views
not dueling monologues	*is* listening and telling with respect

[4] Gecan, *Effective Organizing*, 9.

What the relational meeting is:

a. *Foundational*: the building block of a relational culture of power (power among)
b. *Public action*: discovering and acting on self-interests/values and stories
c. *Intentional*: creating time and space for real conversation and reflection
d. *Art and practice*: a professional and personal spiritual discipline
e. *Conversational*: a mutual exchange with the possibility of conversion on either side
f. *Story oriented*: listening and telling in mutuality
g. *Energy/power building*: a mutual exchange of power forming a public conspiracy

Keys to relational meetings:

- listening and telling
- story
- the "why" question
- agitation/tension
- reflection

APPENDIX 2

A MATRIX OF ORGANIZATION SHIFT AND LEADERSHIP

Leadership shift chart

	Servant	**Manager**	**Ideologue**	**Authoritarian**	**Organizer**
Mode of operation	Meets needs	Runs the ship	Bias	My way	Relational/ strategic
Strategy	React	Org. chart / calendar	Issue	From above	Cultivates vision/leaders
Relationship to members	Helper, listener	Slot filler, servicer	Salesperson	Superior/ subordinate	Mentor
Center	Needs	Tasks and programs	Cause	Hierarchy	Building relationships
Vision	Others' expectations	Maintenance	Vision only	Institution as it is	Concrete vision practices
Institution	Locus of individual relationships	Service provider	Place to recruit	My kingdom or queendom	Threat as opportunity
Mindset	Friend	Marketer, technical	True believer	King/queen	Artist
World	Personal only	Organiza-tional only	World only	Rule or be ruled	Public and private, world as it is ... world as it ought to be
Tools	Time, presence	Meetings and activities	Passion	Meetings	Reflection, questions, one-to-ones, tension, death

Spend some meditation time on this chart. Where do you see your leadership style? Are you where you want to be? If not, how do you want to shift? What would it take for you and others to shift?

APPENDIX 3

CENTRAL CITY 2000 TASK FORCE

Mr. Robert Ridgely, Chair	CEO, Northwest Natural Gas and President, Oregon Business Council
Hon. Vera Katz	Mayor, City of Portland
*Hon. Earl Blumenauer	Commissioner, City of Portland
Mr. Robert Ames	Developer, President First Interstate Bank
Mr. Baruti Artharee	Director, State Housing Department, and Metro Exposition Recreation Commissioner
Dr. Jack Bierwirth	Superintendent, Portland School District
Mr. Frederick Buckman	CEO, PacifiCorp
Hon. Michael Burton	Executive Officer, Metro
Mr. John Eskildsen	President, US Bank
**Ms. Peggy Fowler	Senior VP, Portland General Electric
Mr. Henry Hewitt	Managing Partner, Stoel Rives Law Firm, and Chair, Oregon Transportation Commission
Dr. Peter Kohler	President, Oregon Health Sciences University
Ms. Betty Lee	President, Chin's Import-Export
Dr. Judith Ramaley	President, Portland State University
Mr. Richard Reiten	Chief Operating Officer, Northwest Natural Gas

**Mr. John Russell	President, Russell Development
Mr. Vern Ryles	President, Popper's Supply
Mr. Howard Shapiro	Chair, Housing Authority of Portland
**Mr. Carl Talton	Chair, Portland Development Commission
Mr. Ronald Timpe	CEO, Standard Insurance
Ms. Barbara Walker	Open Space Advocate
Mr. Tom Walsh	General Manager, Tri-Met
Mr. Steven Siegel	Executive Director, Central City 2000 Task Force

* Resigned from task force when elected to US Congress.
** Added to task force in 1996.

APPENDIX 4

SUSTAINABLE WORKS

On December 4, 2008, two hundred MACG leaders initiated a plan to respond with a triple-bottom-line opportunity to a triple-pronged threat:

- How can energy costs that pressure our families and institutions be reduced?
- How might local career jobs be created to support living wages in the midst of economic collapse?
- What might be done concretely to respond in scale to the global climate-change crisis?

The answer: Sustainable Works.

Sustainable Works, already piloted in Spokane and when brought to scale in Portland, Seattle/Tacoma, and Spokane, can retrofit hundreds of thousands of existing buildings, reducing energy costs by 30–50 percent, decreasing global greenhouse gas emissions proportionally while creating thousands of living wage, local, career-path jobs that can never be outsourced.

This is the vision laid out by MACG leader Cherry Harris, Operating Engineers Local 701, at the assembly on December 4, 2008, at St. Andrew Church. The capacity crowd heard the stories from the many angles of this issue. An apprentice whose job has become a lifeline said, "There's a lot of talk about a new economy nowadays. Last time we talked about a new economy, we saw mills close down. This is why it's critical that any 'new economy' and 'green stimulus' mean family wages and jobs for carpenters. 'Cause it isn't enough to have a job if you're making McDonald's wages."

A single mom explained how her family took a vote last winter to decide which three months to have heat because of the cost of heating oil. Delegates listened intently as a leader from St. Andrew reminded us of the dire consequences of doing nothing in response to global warming and encouraged us to think of the generations to come.

MACG leaders responded with letters of intent and pledges to find apprentices, to support them or educate members on global climate change, or to participate in the political work of changing policies to make the triple bottom line work in Oregon. Multnomah County commissioner Jeff Cogen pledged his support for a triple-bottom-line approach and to use county resources, both technical and financial, to bring Sustainable Works to scale. Michael Armstrong of Portland's Office of Sustainable Development also pledged his support in partnership with MACG. City or county bonding authority may be a critical piece of funding this effort. Steve Lacey of the Energy Trust of Oregon, the entity responsible for energy efficiency from the utility side, promised his continued support for the triple-bottom-line program outlined in the regional Sustainable Works document and pledged his technical and financial support for the Oregon effort.

With the possibility of economic stimulus funds in addition to local and state funding, Sustainable Works is poised to be a new New Deal. It's about jobs—quality, living-wage jobs with apprenticeship ladders from underserved communities. It's about reducing energy costs. It's about responding to global warming. It's about a triple-bottom-line response to a triple-pronged threat.

ACKNOWLEDGMENTS

I WANT TO THANK THE LEADERS, MEMBERS, INTERNS, AND FRIENDS OF Redeemer Lutheran Church whose patience, endurance, courage, stubbornness (otherwise known as steadfastness), persistence, and ability to let go and let God astound me. Special gratitude to mentors Dick Harmon, Joe Chrastil, Rev. Michael Keys, and Sister Antoinette Traeger, OSB, and to those leaders who most closely dreamed, prayed, strategized, reflected, acted, and evaluated over and over through the years. Most especially, I want to acknowledge Nancy Phelps, Lois Jordahl, and Rev. Joan Lepley, all longtime members of Redeemer. I'm deeply grateful for the colleagues and leaders in POP, MACG, and IAF NW who accompanied, taught, and worked with me through many difficult times. I'm deeply indebted to the Benedictine Priory at Mount Angel and the Trappist Abbey in Carlton, Oregon, for many spiritual retreats, workshops, and accompaniment. I am thankful for my association with IAF over nearly thirty years as well as sister networks as I've encountered. I want to thank Peggy Lindquist, Buddhist teacher, friend, and colleague, who helped shape and edit the initial manuscript for this book prior to submission to Fortress Press. I want to recognize the Louisville Institute for providing a Pastoral Study Grant and a Pastoral Excellence Network grant, 2014–2016, to further my learning and reflection in transformational leadership. I also am indebted to the Collegeville Institute for a Pastoral Writing Seminar in 2017 that provided encouragement and writing support for this book. Finally, I appreciate the many places I found shelter to think and write, including Holden Village, Menucha Retreat Center, and Ocean Front Cabins, Oceanside, Oregon, to name a few.

INDEX

Page numbers in italics refer to figures and tables.